In the Shadow
of the Midnight Sun

In the Shadow of the Midnight Sun

Contemporary
Sami Prose and Poetry

Edited and introduced
by Harald Gaski

Davvi Girji o.s. 1996

Acknowledgements:
Davvi Girji o.s. would like to acknowledge the authors and their publishers for granting permission to reproduce their texts. We are also grateful to the Sami Cultural Council for its economic support of the project. But we are most in debt to the translators, among whom Edi and Roland Thorstensson should be especially mentioned. Without their gracious assistance this anthology would have been much longer in the making.

Computer typeset by Davvi Girji o.s., Kárášjohka, Norway
Printed by Bjørkmanns Trykkeri AS, Alta, Norway

ISBN 82-7374-309-8

Preface

This is the first extensive anthology of contemporary Sami literature in English. It contains short stories, excerpts from novels, and poetry and is intended to present a varied picture of what Sami authors have written during this century. All four countries in which the Sami live are represented in the anthology, which also includes a comprehensive introduction, intended to provide the reader with background on Sami literary history and to place each text in a context. Introducing each new text is also a brief biographical note about its author.

Most of the texts in the anthology were originally written in Sami, the remainder in Norwegian. Some of the texts have been published previously in Sami/Norwegian bilingual editions. I have checked all the translations against the original Sami work to ensure that the English version is as close to the proto-text as possible. A few Sami words and expressions have been left untranslated in order to retain some of the esthetic qualities of the original texts and also to give the reader a chance to hear the Sami voice inherent in the language. The meaning of these Sami words and expressions should be clear from the context in which they appear. Each translation is of course to be looked upon as a first interpretation of the text; nonetheless, it is my wish that this anthology will contribute to an increased knowledge of and interest in Sami literature internationally. There has been a tremendous rise in the publication of Sami literature in recent decades, and more is being translated now than ever before.

Ever since the world's various indigenous peoples began turning their efforts to cooperative endeavors in the 1970s, the Sami have participated actively in the struggle to make these peoples' and their own voice heard. Art and literature have always played an important role in this endeavor. Therefore, the time for Sami literature to join world literature is past due. By making it available in English, I hope that a wider circle of readers will be reached. I hope as well that this anthology will fill the gap in the availability of works on Sami literature at universities and colleges around the world offering courses on Scandinavian and Sami culture. Although Sami issues have for too long been relegated to the shadows, there is no darkness during the season of the midnight sun....

Harald Gaski

Contents

Introduction

Sapmi

The Sami are a people who live in four nations, inhabiting vast areas in Scandinavia, northern Finland, and northwestern Russia, from the Kola Peninsula in the northeast to the regions of Dalarna, Sweden, and Femunden, Norway, in the south. In Sami language this region is called Sapmi, which denotes the area where Sami people live, the Sami habitat, so to speak. It is difficult to provide an exact total population figure, since the choice to identify oneself as a Sami is an individual one. It is assumed, however, that altogether there are about 50,000 Sami, the majority of whom live in Norway. The word Sami comes from the Sami's own name for themselves, "sámit" or "sápmelaččat". In earlier times in Norway, they were referred to as "Lapps" or "Finns", but today the term "Sami" is increasingly used in the Nordic countries and internationally; it is, for instance, the accepted name within the worldwide indigenous people's movement, in which the Sami take active part.

The old Sami social organization was based upon a *siida* system in which various hunting groups together formed the basis for a larger democratic communal unit, i.e., a village or a district cooperative. Settlement was based on ecological adaptation and migration according to the availability of resources. Thus, most *siidas* operated with several seasonal camps, each located where use could be made of whatever natural resources were most abundant at any given time. Presumably, the *siida* system and the Sami's natural ability to move from areas where resources were no longer available

9

were factors in the avoidance of confrontations between the Sami and Norwegians once intense colonization had begun. In order to avoid conflict, the Sami withdrew to another of their campsites. When they no longer had several places to which to escape, however, the Sami usually had to simply give up. They were left powerless to resist the form of government which the colonists introduced and relied on, but which was foreign to themselves. The new laws brought by the intruders made no allowances whatsoever for Sami tradition or sense of justice.

Colonization began along the coast as early as in the Middle Ages, but was intensified in the 18th century. As time went on, it spread into the fjord areas and up the rivers. As a result, the Sami gradually lost their autonomy. In fact, even in earlier times, the Sami had been subjected to both raids by bands of marauders and taxation by neighboring peoples. Some groups of Sami were actually taxed by three different countries: Norway–Denmark, Sweden–Finland, and Russia.

The idea behind colonization was not simply to seize new territory and more resources, however. In Norway's case, for example, it was also a way to spread Norwegian language and culture to the Sami, so that it could be more justifiably said that these were "Norwegian" Sami and therefore this part of the kingdom belonged to Norway – not to Sweden or Russia, who also laid claim to the same territory. Thus, the policy of assimilation followed colonization like a shadow. It was not enough that the Sami had to relinquish rights to their own land, they were supposed to renounce their own language and culture as well. Assimilation meant that the Sami should be remolded into Norwegians, Swedes, or Finns. Use of the Sami language was not to be encouraged in any way; in fact, its use was forbidden in all but a few isolated situations. Hence, to be a Sami entailed no advantages, only problems. For example, there existed for some time a legal provision which stated that no one could purchase land in Finnmark, the county with the largest Sami population, unless he could speak Norwegian. Furthermore, teachers in the Sami regions of the country were granted wage increases in proportion to the number of Sami school children they had managed to get to stop speaking the Sami language.

The Sami language

The Sami language is divided into several different dialects: Eastern, Northern, Lule, and Southern Sami. The differences between these dialects are so great that a Southern Sami and a Northern Sami can not automatically understand each other. Without question, the largest linguistic sub-group speaks the Northern Sami dialect, which is used more often than any other in conjunction with official Sami matters. Several orthographies have existed over the years. Today's Northern Sami orthography, which is in use in Norway, Sweden and Finland, is from 1979.

The Sami language belongs to the Finno-Ugric branch of the Uralic family of languages. Its wealth of derivative suffixes has made relatively simple the construction of easily recognizable words for the new concepts and objects that modern life has introduced. Thus, rather than simply accepting Norwegian and foreign loan words, the relatively puristic Sami language policy has made both preferable and possible the incorporation of many new Sami expressions into everyday vocabulary through a vigorous use of media and public education.

Sami is exceedingly rich in words describing nature, animal life, land formations, snow, and other things that have been important in connection with fishing and hunting. It also has an extensive vocabulary for designating kinship, which of course explains something about the close personal relationships that have existed within Sami society. Today, a number of these concepts are being lost, because the way of life is undergoing change.

The yoik tradition

Sami literature has its foundations in an old oral literary legacy maintained by skillful narrators and singers. Prose literature can draw from an invaluably rich treasure trove of story and fairy tale, while yoik poetry has tremendous significance for the development of modern Sami poetry. Yoik poetry has provided a native tradition from which contemporary writers can proceed in exciting and creative ways.

Yoik, from the Sami word *juoigan*, is the Sami form of musical expression. Traditionally, the yoik has played an important role in creating a feeling of unity within the group. It has reinforced a Sami's identity by allowing him or her to feel a sense of belonging in a family and society. In the old Sami society, when a person had received a yoik, he or she was looked upon as a member of the community. One might say that the yoik served the same function as baptism and confirmation does today.

The yoik was also tied to the old religion, both as a medium, in the spiritual sense, and as a means used by the shaman in his rituals. The shaman, or *noaidi*, as he was called in the Sami language, was the group's or tribe's wise man. He could heal illnesses, and he could prophesy with the help of his magic drum, which, along with places of sacrifice, was among the holiest of all objects in the old Sami mythology. The yoik was used to draw the shaman into a trance, so that his spirit could wander freely and gain the wisdom he otherwise could not find. Moreover, the yoiks contained central ideas regarding the Sami's view of themselves and of their surroundings. That is, the yoik provided important information for not only a positive self-awareness but also for survival.

Personal yoiks, which today comprise the best-known genre, generally have a musical arrangement as their main element, the words being merely an addition that serves to further describe the person. Both the musical and the verbal portrait of the subject are usually short, concise, striking characterizations. The yoik can be revised or expanded, should the subject change or become something other than that which the community had expected of him or her. In reality, the yoik is not *about* a person, it actually *is* the person – this, too, a sign of just how close the connection between the subject and the musical portrayal is perceived to be.

The oldest Sami poetry consists, then, of yoik texts in the form of short love poems, longer myths, and poetic narratives. The two best-known are those which Sami theological student Olaus Sirma (ca. 1650-1719) wrote down as he remembered them and gave to Professor Johannes Schefferus, who published a book about the Sami in 1673, *Lapponia*. Written in Latin, the book was relatively quickly translated into several European languages, and thus the two poems became known far beyond the borders of Sapmi; in a way they preceded Europe's Age of Romanticism. The poems are called "Moarsi fávrrot" and "Guldnasaš". In both, the woman is absent and the man expresses his deep love for her. In the first poem, he dreams about various ways by which to come to her; for she is far away, and in those days there were few means for rapid transportation. The young man expounds the efforts to which he is willing to go in order to reach his beloved, and he doesn't hesitate to mention the ties that might bind them together. It is apparent, of course, that he has let the girl wait for quite some time while he figures himself out. Now she is clearly tired of waiting for this man who is so full of sweet promises but still in the wind's power, "bártni miella lea biekka miella" ["the boy's will is the wind's will"]. It appears that the man is forced to choose between his affinity with the wind – that which is free to touch everyone – and his own hesitation and procrastination, which could actually lead to his losing his beloved. Towards the end of the poem, it looks as though he has decided to go to his sweetheart, and that is where the next poem picks up: at the start of his journey.

While "Moarsi fávrrot" was clearly set in the summertime, in "Guldnasaš" it is already winter. Thus, the first poem can serve as a commentary to the second; in other words, it has taken quite a while for the man to finally decide to go to his sweetheart. In "Guldnasaš", however, he is on his way. Moreover, once he has reached a decision, his inner conflicts are no longer so pronounced. Now what is most important is that his draft reindeer maintains a good speed and that nature doesn't interfere with the journey. We must keep in mind, here, that this story was originally told at a time when it was accepted that the natural world had a soul, and that the will of the gods and of people could have an influence on nature. Therefore, it was important that one sing a yoik asking difficult mountain passes, ice on the lakes, and snow on the marshes to treat the traveler well.

Among the longer epic yoiks that were transcribed at the beginning of the 19th century – aside from the purely mythical texts – there are yoiks that tell of the Sami people's history, of their settlement in Sapmi, and of conditions that existed in the oldest times. In addition to these, we find religious songs connected with the shamanistic form of religion, as well as purely romantic poetry, comic songs, and other songs about a variety of experiences of which people took special note and upon which a yoik could be based. Some yoiks also contain as well unambiguous political viewpoints regarding the process of colonization to which the Sami had been and were being subjected by the surrounding nations.

Images are extremely important in the Sami's old epic poetry. Particularly elaborate are hidden messages conveyed in the more rebellious songs from the period of colonization. The Sami of that time no doubt feared being understood by any public officials who had acquired a little knowledge of their language and might happen to hear one of their songs. Therefore, they avoided the use of direct language and concealed implied messages in subtle texts; only the initiated could get the points being made. This means of communication served at least two purposes at once: on the superficial level, it contained a harmless tale of various events in the lives of the Sami, while its underlying message to the Sami audience conveyed a call to resist cultural suppression and assimilation.

A part of the Sami's old epic poetry appears to have abandoned its poetical form as it was handed down from generation to generation; it has become more akin to fairy tale or myth. There are examples to support this, one of the most exciting of which is the poem about the Sun's children. The sun, of course, has always been an important force for the Sami, just as it has for so many other peoples around the world. But to our ancestors it seemed very special in that it disappeared entirely for two months during the polar winter night, only to remain in the sky – never setting, sleeping, or resting – during the summer months. The sun has always stood for the goodness in existence, and those Sami who can trace their ancestry back to this primeval force have always been blessed with good fortune. Evil forces are represented by the dark side, the shadows, and there has taken place a perpetual struggle between the two since the beginning of time.

Myth and eroticism

One of the most frequently mentioned Sami epic poems is the long work about the Son of the Sun's going courting in the land of the giants. Recorded by the Southern Sami minister Anders Fjellner (1795–1876), its form is reminiscent of other epic poems. It is tightly structured, full of alliteration and parallelisms, and it has a well-developed imagery. It opens with an introduction about the time when there was "a scarcity of women to pair with men" and continues with a description of the Son of the Sun's conception, birth, and childhood. Then the tale itself begins, "Nu leat mii gullan / Sáhka lea beaggán" ["As we have heard it / So it is told"]. Beyond the north star and west of the sun and moon, there is said to be a land of gold and silver, where the mountains are reflected in the sea. The Son of the Sun desires to travel to that place, so he gathers his best men and sets out on a journey that will last an entire year.

They pass both the sun and the moon, and at last they reach the land of the giants. There they find the giant's young daughter down by the water, preparing to bathe. Eventually she sets her eyes on the Sun's son and asks him, "Gos don boadát, gean don ozat" ["Where do you come from, whom do you seek?"]. She herself hints at answers meant to frighten the Sun's son into turning back immediately. But he hasn't traveled this far only to return home empty-handed, so he boasts of his strength and states his mission. He wants a friend for life who can comfort and encourage him, guide him, and give him heirs. The giant's daughter is flattered and asks her father for permission to marry the Son of the Sun, but the old one will not part so easily with his only daughter. He wants to match his strength against that of the suitor. The blind giant holds out a finger, challenging his opponent to a pulling contest. His daughter thrusts an iron grapnel into the Son of the Sun's hand, and the old one has to admit that the sinews in the lad's fingers are indeed strong. Then he agrees to the marriage. Meanwhile, the intoxicating beverage that the giant is given goes straight to his head, and he rages until he once again has calmed down enough to perform the ceremony. This is carried out ritually on the skin of a whale, the king of the sea. Blood is mixed and knots are tied, all elements of a ritual of mythological origin.

As a dowry the giant's daughter receives great boulders from the golden cliffs along the beach. They are brought on board the Son of the Sun's ship. The giant's daughter removes her maiden's slippers. She hides away her second mother's menstrual napkin, which signifies that she is grown now and ready to become a mother. (Second mother refers to one of the goddesses who play a central role in caring for the home and the well-being of the family.) She receives a secret key and has three chests carried out from a sod hut that was specially built to serve as the resting place of youth. The first chest is blue, the second red, and the third white. Besides these, she takes along the cloth with which she was washing herself at the water's edge when the Sun's son arrived in the land of the giants. In the cloth there are three knots tied in the names of the three goddesses, Máttaráhkká, Sáráhkká, and Uksáhkká. These knots symbolize three forces of wind, from breeze to gale, which are unleashed when the knots are untied.

But when the brothers of the giant's daughter return from hunting seals, whales, and walruses, they discover that their sister is gone. "Whose odor of sweat was so sweet / Who smelled the scent of her bosom / To whom did our sister give her hand?" they ask their father, who answers, "Beaivvi bárdni, borjjus bárdni" ["The son of the Sun, the seafarer"].

17

The brothers return to their oars and take up the chase after the Son of the Sun's ship. Soon they are right behind the fugitives. But then the giant's daughter unties the first knot. The wind rises, fills the sails, and the brothers fall astern. But they do not give up the chase. Soon they are once again about to overtake the fugitives' ship. They holler and threaten, their rage swells, their wrath boils. But the giant's daughter longs only to enter the bridal bed with the Son of the Sun. She unties the second knot, and immediately the wind grows even stronger. The brothers watch as the other boat once again gains the lead. As they close the gap between their ship and that of the Sun's son for the third time, it is no longer sweat but blood that beads their foreheads, and their hands leave impressions on the oars. "Can the boat withstand more wind?" the giant's daughter asks the Son of the Sun. Then she unties the last knot and releases the gale. The ship rolls from side to side, cast among the waves; the mast groans; the giant's daughter seeks cover in the bottom of the boat. Her brothers completely lose track of the ship and are forced to give up the chase. They go ashore to watch from a mountaintop for the Son of the Sun's ship, but there, on the next day, they are struck by the rising sun's rays, and both they and their vessel are turned to stone.

When, at last, the Son of the Sun's ship reaches home, the bridal couple must go through the marriage ceremony that is practiced in the Son of the Sun's kingdom. They are married once again, this time on a bearskin and the hide of a two-year-old female reindeer, and the giant's daughter is transformed into a Sami, "moarsi sámáidahttui". After this, "Her doors are widened / Her room is made larger". This obviously alludes to impregnation, since in the last line it is noted simply, "Thus she bore the Sun's sons." These children were the legendary Gállábártnit, who became the progenitors of the Sami people, and who, upon their death, were not buried in the ordinary way but rather lifted to heaven, because not only were they outstanding hunters, they were also the inventors of skis. Today they make up the constellation Orion's belt.

Both the introduction and the conclusion of the poem have obviously erotic undertones clearly associated with a desire for the continued existence of the Sami people here on earth. There are several levels in the poem which touch upon fertility, reproduction, and sexuality. What may well be most significant of all, however, is that the myth creates a link between the Sami people and the sun. So the poem is in fact meant to legitimize the Sami's right to inhabit Sapmi, that is, the region which they regard as their own.

The first books

The history of Sami literature is relatively short compared to the histories of other cultures' written literatures. The first book written in the Sami language by a Sami and based on material from everyday Sami life, *Muitalus sámiid birra [Turi's book of Lapland,* 1931] by Johan Turi (1854–1936), a reindeer herder, was published in 1910. The book was published simultaneously in Danish, translated by the artist and ethnologist Emilie Demant, who had encouraged Turi to write. Turi's story of the reindeer herding Sami is both realistic and dramatic, and it takes up a definite position against the colonization of Sapmi. Moreover, the book contains a great deal of material about traditional Sami customs, beliefs, and folk medicine. It also provides historical background for a number of legends about such events as the raids carried out in Sapmi by such bands of marauders as the Tjudis, as vividly retold in the Sami feature film, *Ofelaš [Pathfinder]*. In the story appearing in this anthology, Turi tells us how a yoik might come about among the Sami, and, true to his narrative style, he fashions his story into an exciting account, laced with romantic intrigue.

Only two years after Turi's book appeared, journalist and teacher Anders Larsen (1870–1949) published through his own company in Christiania [Oslo] the first novel to appear in the Sami language, *Beaivi-álgu* [Daybreak], whose central theme is the author's belief in Sami self-respect. *Beaivi-álgu* is really a simple book, a bit reminiscent of popular fiction. Still, it says something important to the Sami reader. It is psychological in the sense that it allows the reader not only to take part in telling the story but also to go further with it. A Sami's reading of *Beaivi-álgu* never stops where the author ceases to speak, for the story has above all contributed to a process of associative co-creation based on the reader's own experiences. One discovers that little has changed in the past 80 years, and even if one doesn't exactly identify personally with Ábo's story, reading it awakens feelings and attitudes, so that the book gains importance as a key to a clearer understanding about the Sami's situation as a minority group.

Beaivi-álgu says something about the consequences of Norwegianization and thus elucidates some of the reasons for the Sami language and culture's gradually being assigned such low status, even among many Sami. Larsen, however, is out to do more than simply explain a state of affairs; he also offers a vision of something better, a utopia toward which to strive. It was Larsen's intention to address the issues of his day by using creative writing as a means to express his view of contemporary society. In many ways, his book is an extension of his perhaps even more important contribution as a cultural figure and Sami political pioneer through the newspaper he edited from 1904 to 1911, *Sagai Muittalægje*, which, among other things, served as a mouthpiece for Isak Saba, who in

1906 became the first Sami elected to the Norwegian National Assembly.

Matti Aikio (1872–1929) was Sami and could speak the Sami language, but he chose to write in Norwegian. Aikio produced six novels and wrote a great number of newspaper and magazine articles. He made his debut during the time when efforts to Norwegianize the Sami were most intense; in contrast to Anders Larsen, however, who took a stand against the policy of assimilation, Aikio supported it, because he felt that the Sami were so racially intermixed that the genuinely Sami culture had already been lost, or at least was about to be. He saw a certain amount of hope for the survival of his people's former pride through reindeer herding as a way of life, but he saw nothing positive in the coastal Sami fishing and farming culture. Making his home in Oslo – far from Sapmi – for most of his adult life, Aikio still was regarded by his contemporaries as the Sami's poet.

In spite of Aikio's wholehearted support of the government's assimilation policy, most noticeably expressed in his newspaper and magazine articles, one can detect slightly different attitudes in some of his other more purely literary works. This is particularly true in the novel *Bygda på elveneset* [The River Spit Village], published in 1929, the year of Aikio's death. Here, people of Sami, Finnish, and Norwegian ethnic background live in harmony, and the novel includes several passages where Sami esthetic values are presented as representative and beautiful and manifested by not only well-made handicraft but also practical work, such as driving a reindeer-drawn sled or punting a river boat, as described in the excerpt selected for this anthology.

When Aikio died, the text was still in an unfinished state. The final editing has been done by Regine Norman, who was also from the North but lived in Oslo .

From tundra to desk

During the years between the world wars, efforts to shape a homogeneous Norwegian population were further intensified, creating problems for all forms of Sami political activity. No books in the Sami language were published in Norway, with the exception of an important volume compiled and edited by a researcher, J. K. Qvigstad's Lappiske eventyr og sagn (1927–29) [Sami Folktales and Legends]. In Finland, Hans Aslak Guttorm (1906–1992) made his debut in 1940 with a collection of poetry and short stories, Koccam spalli [Rising Wind]. Guttorm had relegated his earlier manuscripts to the desk drawer, where they remained until the 1980s, when they were published as a series. The short story "Winter Night" is from Guttorm's first published book, and it describes the dramatic struggle between a reindeer herder and wolves that are ravaging the herds. In this realistic story, which sends cold shivers down the reader's spine, the wolves attack both the reindeer and the herder's dogs.

Guttorm is in many ways the connecting link between tradition and the new Sami writers who have established themselves in recent decades. Indeed, he was honored by his colleagues in the Sami Writers' Association with their recommendation for the Nordic Council's Prize for Literature in 1984, the first year in which the Sami, together with the people of Greenland and the Faeroe Islands, were granted the opportunity to nominate books for this prize.

Oktyabrina Voronova (1934–1990) is the only Sami from Russia represented in this anthology. She wrote most of her works in Russian, because no orthography had been developed for her dialect, Ter Sami, until 1982. She published three volumes of poetry in Russian. *Yealla* [Life], her only book in the Sami language, was published immediately after her death. It is from this book that the poems in this anthology are taken.

Ter Sami is one of four Sami dialects found in the Russian part of the Sami region. This dialect is now in danger of dying out. Not much literature in the Sami language has been published in Russia thus far, because a strict policy of assimilation was imposed on the Sami during the Soviet period. Moreover, there have been very few individuals able to translate from Russian Sami to either the Scandinavian languages or English. During the 1930s, reindeer herding in the Soviet Union underwent forced collectivization. Only those Sami who continued to tend the herds were allowed to remain on the tundra; all others were moved into towns and villages, particularly to Lovozero in the central Kola Peninsula. This event has had negative consequences for the approximately two thousand Sami who live in Russia. Since the end of the Cold War, Russia's opening up to the West has not brought noticeably improved conditions for the Sami, since the Sami are now losing their hunting and trapping rights to wealthy foreign investors, who buy up exclusive rights to turn large tracts of land into tourist attractions. These entrepreneurs rent out fishing privileges at such high prices that the Sami have no chance to compete and therefore lose their claim to their own territory and to make use of local resources.

Oktyabrina Voronova came from a small place in the eastern part of the Kola Peninsula with the poetic name "with the eyes turned toward the forest." During the 1960s, the village was shut down and people moved away, because the authorities said that there were no possibilities for development there. (The area, however, has a wealth of petroglyphs carved into granite rock.) Voronova continued her education in Lovozero and studied at the Herzen Pedagogical Institute in St. Petersburg. She later worked at the library in Revda, where, at a memorial ceremony held in her honor in 1993, a prize for Sami literature was established in her name.

Voronova's writing is reminiscent of Paulus Utsi's observations of a life close to nature, perhaps not so amazing in light of the fact that they both had their backgrounds on the mountain plateaus and tundra. In Voronova's imagery the metaphor is bound to familiar Sami figures, such as "The snow is light / soft as a reindeer calf" or "The sun's rays are like reins/ two beams, sled tracks."

Today, more literature is published in the Sami language in Russia than once was the case, but most recent books are published by the Sami company Davvi Girji in Norway, in a cooperative effort between Sami people in Russia and Norway that is primarily made possible by Norwegian financial support. The texts are rendered in both Russian Sami orthography and in Northern Sami, the latter being by far the most common Sami dialect of all. Mostly children's books and collections of fairy tales have been published thus far.

Ensnaring the language

Sami literature first began to flourish in the 1970s, a period of increased Sami cultural and societal activity during which advances were made in the struggle for Sami rights and a number of important institutions were founded. At the end of the decade, the first artists' associations were formed and the first Sami publishing company saw the light of day, which meant that the threshold was lowered a bit, encouraging Sami writers to dare come forth with their manuscripts. Sami literature became established as a university subject during the course of the 1980s, and, in recent years, both translations and anthologies of Sami literature have appeared in other languages. This anthology, however, is the first comprehensive presentation in English of a wide spectrum of Sami literature.

Of all the Sami art forms, it is perhaps literature that has had to strive against the greatest odds. Anyone can listen to music or look at a picture without having special qualifications to do so. Without the ability to read, however, no one can have direct access to literature. There are still many Sami who have never been educated in their own language. Others have lost their language through Norwegianization and assimilation and can experience Sami literature only in translation. But there is little money for publishing both original editions and translations. The market is so small that no company can hope to recover its costs through sales. In order for a book in the Sami language to be published, it must be almost completely financed by the government.

One of the most prominent Sami cultural figures to emerge during the new revitalization at the end of the 1960s was Paulus Utsi (1918-1975). He combined his job as a teacher of *duodji* (handicraft) at the Sami Folk High School in Jokkmokk, Sweden, with writing poetry. Utsi had a plan in his writing: He wanted to capture the language, to catch it in the very snares of language itself. Utsi published two collections of poetry, *Giela giela* (1974) and *Giela gielain* (1980), the latter appearing posthumously, with his wife, Inger, as co-author. In an interview, Utsi once explained that the Sami used to write in the snow, and that made him think of writing poetry. Perhaps it is precisely the transitoriness of this type of writing that he had in mind when, in one of his poems, he compares the threatened state of the Sami way of life with ski tracks across the open tundra that the wind wipes out even before the next day has dawned.

Like other cultural work, writing fiction as a creative process has only recently become means for gaining any particular social status among the Sami. How to write was considered worth knowing – a valuable skill for carrying out business transactions, for example – but it was mainly the others, the non-Sami majority, who reaped the benefits of their ability to write. Even if Sami parents did encourage their children to do well in school in order to succeed in the new society, the perception of real work was still associated with manual labor and the Biblical edict, "In the sweat of thy face shalt thou eat bread." But Paulus Utsi understood that his people, too, had to learn new techniques and that, in many fields, they would have to resort to the "arts" of the others in order to be heard and taken seriously. Utsi stressed both aspects of writing: its utilitarian value as a means for both learning and earning income, on the one hand; on the other, its esthetic dimension – writing as an art form, as literature, which in its own way can open up completely different avenues for understanding and communication than can factual prose. Utsi wanted the Sami to preserve their own language as the minority's own voice, but he also wanted them to learn the language of the majority in order to expose the majority's linguistic manipulation of the Sami. In other words, they should become aware of language as a trap with which one could ensnare, but also in which one could be ensnared.

In Sami tradition, anyone who discovers something new must also demonstrate that the discovery is significant, viable, and of value. Therefore, Paulus Utsi was cautious when he set out to write poetry, first submitting some of his poems to the journal *Samefolket*, which is published in Sweden. Next, he wrote a small cycle of poems, made himself heard here and there, gained recognition, became someone from whom people wanted to hear more. And, then, suddenly, the time was ripe to publish his first collection of poetry, *Giela giela* [Capture the Language] – that is to say, a call for gaining control over the language. In his second collection, *Giela gielain* [Capture the Language in a Snare], he becomes more explicit about his intentions. It is the language that he wants to capture in the snare, and the mechanism he will use – the snare – is language itself; for in Sami the same words are used for learning languages and checking a snare: "oahppat giela" can mean both "learning a language" and "looking to see if there is anything caught in the snare."

Trekways of the Wind

Nils-Aslak Valkeapää (1943–) shares Utsi's multidimensional view of language and art. He is referred to by many, therefore, as a multimedia artist. He made his debut as an author in 1974, the same year as did Paulus Utsi. As a musician as well as a painter and poet, Valkeapää reaches for the special quality in that which is Sami. His concrete wordplay can at times go from being "tracks in word form" to being actual drawings of animal tracks across the pages of a book of poetry, where the tracks are not only the signs that remain after the words, but also – and perhaps more importantly – tracks to follow in order to reach a deeper understanding.

Nils-Aslak Valkeapää won the Nordic Council's Prize for Literature in 1991 with his book *Beaivi, Áhčažan* [The Sun, My Father], whose title alludes to the myth about the Sami as the children of the Sun. The book is an amalgamation of old photographs and newly-written lyrical poetry that ties together the past and present, the documentary and the fictional, in a form that is innovative and creative and with a content that unites visual images, words, and music. It provides at once an expression of Sami cultural history and the richness of language. Its words' double and multiple meanings inspire the reader to reflect. The photographs illustrate various aspects of the Sami people's lives and history and comprise an enormous body of documentary material, which the author spent six years collecting in Scandinavia, Europe, and the United States.

Nonetheless, the pictures are not primarily documentary. Rather, they are arranged by a lyrical poet who wishes us to discover the pictures' intrinsic poetry through the composition of his work at the same time as he wishes to unveil his idea to give expression to the interplay between the verbal and the visual. By observing the photographs in the book, the reader forms associations which the poet, in turn, uses as background for taking us further along into the richly metaphorical world of language, which does not necessarily have to be less real than the concrete world seen through the camera's lens. Thus, *Beaivi, Áhčažan* can also be seen as a defense of the meaning of poetry in today's society. Perhaps poetry, too, must seek new forms of expression and find new allies, in order to reach out to the reader in this age so dominated by visual media.

In a purely artistic sense, Valkeapää continues the idea from *Ruoktu váimmus* (1985) *[Trekways of the Wind, 1994]*, but he goes a step further by testing new forms for combining words and images, visual impressions and associations, expressions and content. In one poem, the words appear to be spread across the page without any apparent connection, until we discover from the meaning of the words that they actually represent an entire herd of reindeer. Each word stands for a reindeer, and each word is different from the others. In the Sami language there are innumerable ways to describe reindeer, such as according to their sex, age, or variations in their appearance. For the non-Sami reader, the words will have very little meaning, even when translated. For the Sami reader who doesn't know the terminology, the text will remain difficult to see as anything more than a typographical layout representing a reindeer herd, even though it is possible to sense something of the poetical

28

in the way in which some of the names are formed. It is by such simple means that Valkeapää elicits the different depths to which different readers can understand a text. If we interpret the broken lines that run from individual words across one page and onto the next, then the whole poem is set in motion – the reindeer herd, too, is obviously on the move.

For this anthology I have chosen the section of *Trekways of the Wind* that has, perhaps, reached further out into the world than any other Sami literature – with the exception of Olaus Sirma's love poem from the 17th century – namely the "My Home Is in my Heart" sequence. In this section we find the classic conflict between the Western ownership-and-exploitation attitude toward nature and a relationship that is based more on a sense of kinship and equality with our immediate surroundings, as expressed in indigenous peoples' respect for nature.

Between tradition and the modern

In the 1970s, women joined the new Sami literary wave, and they have continued to strengthen their position ever since. The most versatile among them is without a doubt Kirsti Paltto (1947–), who writes poetry, short stories, novels, and radio plays for both children and adults. She is also by far the most prolific of any Sami writer. Paltto often places the events in her stories a ways back in time, and she sometimes writes in a style that is related to both traditional storytelling and the modern short story. "Looking Back" is representative of Paltto's style; it is retrospective, the action having taken place some decades earlier. The attitudes described in the story are not found only in the past, however; their remnants exist in today's society to a greater degree than we care to believe.

Paltto has been mindful of the Sami's future in her poetry, where we also find her commitment to international literary trends. One theme in Paltto's poetry is how Sami children will manage to preserve their cultural identity in a future society in which the threats to a distinctive Sami lifestyle will only multiply. She often draws symbols and motifs from Sami mythology, particularly in her children's books, and places these in contrast to the present problems of Sami everyday life. In recent years, Paltto has mainly written novels. One of these, *Guhtoset dearvan min bohccot* [May Our Reindeer Graze in Peace], was nominated for the prestigious Finlandia Prize in 1986.

Rauni Magga Lukkari (1943–) has shown a gradual movement away from a clearly ethnic-emancipatory to a more personal poetry, in which the poet-self's voice rises not so much from her ethnic and cultural background as from her desires and longings as a woman. In her first book, *Jienat vulget* [The Ice Breaks], published in 1980, Lukkari hits upon a number of themes to which she later returns and further develops. By using irony and humor, she gets the reader to observe matters from a fresh perspective. From her portrayal of the deceived woman in *Báze dearvan, Biehtár* [Farewell, Biehtár], via *Losses beaivegirji* (1986) [Dark Journal], in which there are two main female characters – a liberated woman as subject and her oppressed counterpart in an objectified personification of female destiny, whose life is dominated by alienation, superficial modernization, and social isolation – Lukkari has gone on to write about a proud, free woman in *Mu gonagasa gollebiktasat / Min konges gylne klær* (1991) [My King's Golden Clothes]. Here the woman is still divided concerning her relationship with the man, at times uncertain what she should do, but nonetheless more certain of her own worth than were her literary predecessors. "I am no more than halfway. / For the first time now / I am ready to depart. / To begin / my own / journey";

on the other hand: "You / stand in the middle / of my life / like a pillar. / If I fell you / I will be / without feet." This woman is at the same time confident in the power she has over the man, for she says that it is the skill of her eyes and hands that determines for how long her king will sparkle in his golden clothes.

Rauni Magga Lukkari was chosen to be the Sami contender for the Nordic Council's Prize for Literature in 1987 for her *Losses beaivegirji*. She is represented in this anthology by poems selected from her first four volumes of poetry.

Synnøve Persen (1950–) is perhaps recognized first and foremost as a visual artist. Her twofold artistic approach to book production can be noted in the play between text and watercolor illustration, not least of all in her work from 1992, *biekkakeahtes bálggis* [windless path], for which she was nominated for the Nordic Council's literary prize. Here the pictures do not serve primarily to illustrate the poems but rather actually tell their own parallel story, alongside the words. The wholeness achieved in the meeting between two art forms gives the book an extra dimension. The text intimates, insinuates, directs the reading, while the pictures bring home the point with their simple lines and quiet opposition to a single interpretation. In her book, Persen purifies the yoik's poetical brevity and striking expression to an almost minimalistic style, where all that is superficial is pared away, and the poems step forth in the total nakedness of their words, as in "bare trees / search for / the birds" and "silent rooms / fall / leaves."

The book jacket and first illustration show a leaf with clearly visible veins, while the veins are entirely gone in the final picture. The composition of the watercolors throughout the book play upon a contrast between the rounded, labyrinthian versus the disjointed, angular. The rainbow-like interval illustration is introduced with the poem, "soft / soft / lips / open / open / heart," and ends with "the secret of the ocean / moonbeam / kissing you". Under the rainbow's arch swims the poem's "I" in the early light of day. She is called by the night birds to take a chance on something that is only vaguely defined. Both the textual and the visual context clearly imply, however, that it all revolves around a love-encounter, a matter of daring to open oneself to another, as might a starfish. That the reality of a harsh world forces the starfish to close and thrust out its spines in defense is paralleled in the text with a faded summer and bare trees.

In *ábiid eadni* (1994) [the sea's mother], it is again apparent that Persen the visual artist and Persen the writer work in tandem. This no doubt has to do as much with the book's overall design and individual pages as with the interplay between the words' message and the dark, melancholy visual metaphor that is conveyed by the pure black lustrous paper that comprises the entire book – except for the bright red facing pages that occur at the middle of the volume as a shocking contrast to or amplification of the black.

Ever since her debut with *alit lottit girdilit* (1981) [blue birds flying], Persen has distinguished herself as a poet with a sure feel for style, an artist who plays upon poetry's metaphorical nature in her illustrations. Through all three of her books of poetry, Persen insists upon her right to express herself with unbound freedom, insists that her personal artistic objectives will not be relegated to some ethnic or cultural category. Persen refuses to be caged. Art is, in itself, free; hence, each one of us has the right to develop a life design. Persen is represented in this anthology by poems from her first two books.

From storytelling to writing

The selection by Eino Guttorm (1941–) is an excerpt from his novel *Varahuvvan bálgát* (1985) [On Bloodied Paths]. Guttorm's is an allegorical tale about the colonization of Sapmi, told as the story of evil Aleks, who comes to live with the young Sami woman Gáisá and her mother. These women live alone outside of the community and are the objects of some local gossip. None of the rumors about Gáisá are actually true, but they serve to place her and her mother on the margin of society. Aleks sees the possibility to find a niche with them, since he, too, is an outsider.

Eino Guttorm's method for telling this story is much like that of a grandfather telling a legend to his grandchild. As such, *Varahuvvan bálgát* can be seen as Guttorm's attempt at using the oral narrative tradition to create modern literature, a technique that is being discussed worldwide in reference to the problems and challenges that accompany the transition from oral to written culture. Guttorm has written several novels as well as collections of short stories and theatrical scripts. He has also published lyrical poetry. In the excerpt included here, it is Gáisá's mother who stands in the way of Aleks's plans to gain control over her daughter and all that they own.

The contribution by Jovnna-Ánde Vest (1948–) is a chapter from his prize-winning book, *Čáhcegáddái nohká boazobálggis* (1988) [The Reindeer Path Ends at the River Bank], with which he made his debut. This book is something between fiction and a biography of his father. His father, who was killed in an airplane accident on his way to an important Sami conference, was an outsider among his own people, yet somehow a spokesman for them. The author manages to lift the depiction of his father from the usual biography to an artistic portrayal of a man filled with conflict, who lives in the middle of a time when great social, economic, and cultural changes are rapidly taking place in the small Sami communities in the north. This is a time when the automobile, motorcycle, and phonograph appear along the banks of the Tana River – and "Father" in the story is the first to acquire them all. It is also at this time that the local bureaucracy enters into people's everyday lives, so that to hold a post in local government means status and an important say in the direction things will take. Father is involved here, too, but none of this brings him happiness. As time goes on, he is more and more an irritable, frustrated man.

Even in the way he makes use of his immediate surroundings, Father shows himself to be a man who follows his own path. He prefers to walk where others fear to tread. In the forests and mountains, however, he shows another side of himself. He is kind and thoughtful, a man who patiently teaches his children the techniques they will need to know in order to get along in the woods and fields. And he tells stories – not about ten-headed trolls or his life as a soldier on the front, but about small, everyday occurrences that have meaning for people in their own communities. In this excerpt from Vest's book, we are taken along on a trip to pick cloudberries.

Vest, who lives in Paris, has since published two novels dealing with individuals' alienation from their own background and culture. The events and casts of characters in these books are not specifically Sami, but given the fact that the books are written in the Sami language and published by a Sami company, it is reasonable to believe that the author's intended audience is the Sami reading public. Further, it is also quite reasonable to interpret the books' themes as relevant for a discussion of identity and ethnicity both on a personal level and within a social context. Vest can be seen as taking up the legacy left by Matti Aikio from the beginning of this century, where Aikio discusses in a couple of his books what one today might call identity management and alienation.

John Erling Utsi (1952–) is first and foremost known as a journalist, but he has also written a number of short stories and a series of children's programs that have been aired in Scandinavia over Sami radio. John Erling is a younger relative of the poet Paulus Utsi (1918–75), and, like the older Utsi, he has experienced the destructive consequences that damming and regulating rivers can have on both nature and way of life. A recently dammed-up lake provides the gloomy thematic background for the short story selected for inclusion here. The lake is now unrecognizable to the Sami, who have always traveled and fished on it. It is as if the water has gone through a metamorphosis from friend and provider to enemy. The Sami have always believed in an animistic nature, so it is understandable that a dammed lake, with its devastated soul and vengeance, might appear hostile. This story comes from the Sami anthology *Savvon* [Calm], published in 1983.

John Gustavsen (1943–) is represented here by a short story from his first book, *Lille Chicago*, from 1978. "The War Is Over" is a story about two families who are on their way back to their homes in Finnmark in northernmost Norway, after having been forcibly evacuated at the very end of the Second World War. Finnmark, like the rest of Norway, was occupied by German soldiers during the war. The evacuation took place at the order of top officials in Nazi Germany and, together with a scorched earth policy, was designed so that the advancing Red Army would enter deserted territory. Finnmark had, and still has, a relatively heterogeneous population. Sami live both in the interior and in the great coastal fjord districts, and reindeer herders move with their herds to the coast for the summer season. There once existed a rather close cooperation between the various Sami groups. In the short story, references are made to this historical background, but also to some of the tensions that existed between the Sami and the rest of the coastal population.

Gustavsen is otherwise known as a tireless worker for the rights of Sami writers, among other things having been involved in the establishment in 1979 of the Sami Writers' Association, Sámi Girječálliid Searvi, which today is a member of the European Writer's Congress. Gustavsen has also written a play for Beaivváš Sami theater about the author Johan Turi and his relationship with the Danish anthropologist Emilie Demant (later Demant Hatt), without whose support Turi's *Muitalus sámiid birra* might not have come into being.

Modern Sami and new themes

Ellen Marie Vars (1957–) has written several novels for young people and, like authors such as Kerttu Vuolab and Veikko Holmberg, is especially interested in producing reading materials in the Sami language for younger audiences. Vars made her literary debut in 1986 with her novel *Kátjá*, the story of a young Sami girl and her gradual realization of how a lack of consciousness and solidarity among the Sami creates conflicts and hinders betterment. The story's dramatic tension has its roots in the difference in social status allotted the settled and the reindeer-herding Sami, based on which is supposedly the "most" Sami or the "most genuinely" Sami. At the boarding school, Katja is bullied by the children of reindeer herders, because her family does not own reindeer. She also does not get along with the Norwegian school system but nonetheless pursues a higher education.

Kátjá's structure is very reminiscent of Anders Larsen's novel from 1912. Both borrow features from popular literature; in both, the characters are somewhat clichéd. Kátjá, for example, often loses herself in romantic daydreams, which makes her seem passive. At the end of the book, however, she ends up at a Sami meeting in Oslo, where she finally feels accepted and equal.

In *Buot ovddemus jápmet niegut* (1992) [Dreams Die First], we encounter another young girl, whose parents' divorce has a destructive effect on her development. It is especially difficult for her to bear the loss of the close contact with her father that she had enjoyed during her childhood, and this drives the girl into a way of life that undermines her desire to go on living.

The excerpt appearing in this anthology is taken from the section of *Kátjá* that revolves around Kátjá's experiences at the boarding school.

Inger Haldis Halvari (1952–) is primarily an author of children's books, but she has also written several short stories. She often ties childhood memories to the harsher realities of adult life, as in "Little Lake, Hear Me!" Lack of communication and the misinterpretation of signals that leads to larger conflicts are frequent themes in her short stories. These as well as the plain foolishness and repressive attitudes that we meet in this short story belie something about the modern human condition that varies little, whether one is Sami or not.

Aagot Vinterbo-Hohr (1936–) comes from a coastal Sami background. She alludes to her artistic intentions with the title of her first book, *Palimpsest*. The term palimpsest comes from the Greek and means a piece of parchment or other writing material from which the original text has been erased in order to make room for a new text, which can, in turn, be erased and written over.

Written in Norwegian, *Palimpsest* is an intellectual, reflective, and provocative book, simultaneously international and distinctly Sami. The author says, "I read the possibility for a truer story, and I write." The story that she introduces is seen from an educated, intellectual woman's perspective, that of a woman who is the member of a minority society. In this story, Sami cultural knowledge goes hand in hand with theoretical knowledge, and together they put into words a portion of the control mechanisms and dominant relationships that have an oppressive effect on both gender and ethnicity. It is from the parallelisms in the described situations that the book derives its strength; recognition can function on many levels. There are many histories elsewhere in the world similar to that of the Sami, a fact that makes the Sami experiences universal at the same time as they serve to educate the Sami about what to learn from history in general. Here and there, the author uses words and expressions that have been influenced by the Sami language, something which for a Sami reader means that the Sami language can be sensed beneath the surface of the Norwegian text. Toward the end of the book, the Norwegian surface is broken, and the poems of Rauni Magga Lukkari appear in their original Sami form. By holding the palimpsest up to the light, we have brought forth a new Sami text. Perhaps we have also brought forth a long-hidden, dormant Saminess. For in many of the coastal Sami areas, where Norwegianization has had the most time to do its work, it has been believed that the process of de-Samification was completed. But apparently this is not the case.

Palimpsest is a kind of prose poem. It tells a main story by telling many, juxtaposing its own text with others through use of quotations and excerpts as well as subtler allusions. In this way, the author brings out new levels of understanding in the quoted texts by combining them with her own writing; at the same time, she creates an entirely new text. Perhaps this is analogous to being a Sami in today's world. We live in constant interaction with the other people around us; at the same time, we remain something of our own. Yet without the others, our lives would not be as exciting as they are.

The Sami at home and in the world

Marry A. Somby (1953–) made her debut as an author back in 1976 with the first Sami-language children's book, *Ammul ja alit oarbmælli* [Ammul and the Blue Cousin]. She published her first collection of lyrical poetry in 1994, a bilingual edition in Sami and Norwegian, *Mu Apache ráhkesvuohta / Krigeren, elskeren og klovnen* [The Warrior, the Lover, and the Clown]. In her poems, Somby reflects a common indigenous people's perspective more clearly than any Sami writer before her. We find references to other peoples and their symbols in the lyrical poetry of Nils-Aslak Valkeapää and Kirsti Paltto as well, but Marry A. Somby approaches the society she is describing in another way. She takes an active interest in what is the Indians' everyday life today, for better or worse. In spite of the fact that the Sami title of her book, directly translated, is "My Apache Love", the book's theme is not bound to only one tribe. The Inca warrior and Hopi traditions play an important role here, but other mythological and magical concepts are central to an understanding of the poems' content as well, perhaps not least of all to an understanding of the magical reality from which they spring and which they describe. In a way, Somby's poems transcend the boundaries of a purely Sami interpretation; even at their most basic level, they go beyond a single interpretation, as their focus is at one and the same time both wide and narrow, both inclusive and exclusive.

As a writer of prose, Ailo Gaup (1944–) is the poet Somby's male counterpart when it comes to taking old, traditional concepts seriously and using them artistically in a new literary context. Gaup first appeared in 1982 with his book of lyrical poetry, *Joiken og kniven* [The Yoik and the Knife]. He published yet another volume of poetry before coming along in 1986 with *Under dobbel stjernehimmel* [Beneath a Twofold Firmament], a poetic tale. In the latter, Gaup enters the subject area that has since been the most central in his literary universe, the mythological dimension of Sami tradition. In his first novel, *Trommereisen* (1988) *[In Search of the Drum*, 1993], Gaup has his main character, Jon, travel north in order to seek a Sami shaman's drum that is in danger, as well as to gain more knowledge about the drum and how to use it. The excerpt appearing in this anthology is taken from the first chapters of the sequel, *Natten mellom dagene* [Night Between the Days], from 1992, in which Jon once again finds himself in the heart of Sapmi. This time he has traveled northward in order to make his own shaman drum.

Stig Gælok (1961–) is a poet who writes in the Lule Sami dialect, which is spoken by perhaps fewer than one thousand people. Besides this, Gælok belongs to the coastal Sami culture, a way of life that has long been in the shadow of the more exotic reindeer herding culture. When, in 1983, he published his first book of poetry, *O, Oarjjevuodna* [Oh, Oarjjevuodna], it was the first of its kind ever to appear in the language of the Lule Sami. Since then, Gælok has published several more books of poetry, among them "...*ale desti!*" / "...*ikke mer!* " [never again!] in 1992. This book is written as an *armme* – a lament – from a man to his brother, who has had his life's thread cut under dramatic circumstances. In a figurative language reminiscent of the religious metaphors that are peculiar to the local denomination, Læstadianism, Gælok paints, with a perspective that sees beyond one individual's fate, a strong image of sorrow, self-reproach, and longing, as well as of love and faith. In *"Vuonak"* / *"fra fjordene"* (1986) [from the fjords], Gælok sings the praises of the people living along the fjords, the suppressed coastal Sami, in a poetic attempt to strengthen their self-respect and belief in their intrinsic value.

Inger-Mari Aikio (1961–) has brought a fresh, youthful voice to Sami literature with her three works, *Gollebiekkat almmi dievva* (1988) [The Sky Full of Gold-Winds], *Jiehki vuolde ruonas gidda* (1994) [Beneath the Glacier Green Spring], and *Silkeguobbara lákca* (1995) [The Silk Mushroom's Cream]. Included here are selections from her first two books. In *Gollebiekkat almmi dievva*, Aikio is experimental in her expression and breaks the close bond between the poet, the text, and the context that yoik lyrics represented; here she is stylistically innovative and closer to international trends than to Sami literary tradition. Yet a traditional way of expression nearly catches up with her in her ensuing works. She uses a more aphoristic style in her latest volume of poetry, where a kind of resignation seems about to overtake the youthful enthusiasm of her first book.

On the visual level alone, it is a pleasure to page through *Silkeguobbara lákca*, thanks to John Åke Blind's incredibly beautiful pictures, such as icicles that resemble pillars or segments of frozen water that remind one of sculptures or paintings. It is pleasant to note the way in which the photographs and the poems quite clearly compliment one another thematically, for example where some of the poems' cool exteriors are reflected in the cold blue color of the ice. It is woman who always stands in the center of Aikio's poems, with an ironic distance – both from herself, in terms of her own experiences, and from the text – which she uses as a metaliterary medium to process her experiences. Aikio is true to her artistic plan: to objectify romantic encounters and disappointments for the sake of creating literature. The "I" in her poems, however, is no long-suffering woman, broken by men's deceit; she settles the matter in plain words, "lie to me / deceive me / you will be my poems."

Life and art, language and literature, hand in hand – in the Arctic winter as well as in the shadow of the midnight sun…

Johan Turi

Songs of the Sami

Johan Turi (1854–1936) is the classic among all Sami writers. As the author of the first book written in Sami, he holds a special position in the history of Sami literature. Turi was a reindeer herder, born on the the Norwegian side of the border, but because of the regulations that prohibited the Sami from moving their herds across the national borders within Nordkalotten, the northernmost region of Fenno-Scandinavia, he and his family had to settle in the area near Kiruna in northern Sweden. Here Turi became acquainted with the Danish painter and ethnologist Emilie Demant (later Demant Hatt) during her visit to Swedish Sapmi in 1907–1908. In several ways she inspired Johan Turi to become a writer and was also greatly responsible for the fact that *Muitalus sámiid birra* appeared 1910 in a parallel edition in Sami and Danish.

*T*HE SAMI WAY OF SINGING is called 'yoiking'. It is an art form with which to remember other people. Some are remembered with hate, some with love, and others with sorrow. And the yoik works in such a way that when a talented yoiker sings, it is so good to hear that people are moved, but when the yoikers are the kind who swear and threaten to butcher the reindeer and even kill the owner, then it is terrible to listen to.

There are also yoiks dedicated to nature and to animals, to the wolf and the reindeer, both tame and wild. Here is a *luohti* to the reindeer:

Silke-njávvi,
the one with the soft silk hair
voya voya nana nana
they dashed away like the beams of the sun
voya voya nana nana
the little calves grunted
voya voya nana nana
the herd moves like the swiftest streams
voya voya nana nana.

The following story explains the function of the yoik.

Two young women are talking to each other. One of them says to the other, "Make a yoik for Niillas, the one you love!" All the girls think that Niillas is a handsome fellow, and all of them want him, and that's why they sing about him so often. A yoik of that kind is called a *luohti*. The girl then begins her Niillas-*luohti*:

"Voya voya nana nana,
what a man, so stalwart,
so handsome to look at,
voya voya nana nana –
when he runs, it's as if he had wings
voya voya nana nana."

Then she says to the other girl, "Can't you sing a yoik for the one you love!"

The other answers, "I don't have a loved one!"

"Oh, I'm sure you do," the first girl continues.

"Who do you think that would be, then?"

"I think it's Máhtte."

"No, I don't think Máhtte is interested in me. He has someone who's better than I," she answers.

This second girl is clever. She doesn't tell that there is someone she loves, and that it is Niillas. Therefore she wants to fool the other one to reveal whether she thinks she is going to get Niillas.

But Niillas himself had never considered taking the first girl. He was only interested in the clever one; therefore, he often yoiked her *luohti* thus:

> Voya voya nana nana,
> this fair girl, this beautiful one,
> she's so quick and smart,
> voya voya nana nana
> quick and smart,
> the finest in this *siida*,
> voya voya nana nana.

When Niillas saw this bright girl, however, he stopped yoiking. But this girl, whose name is Elle, yoiked in such a way that Niillas would hear it, a yoik saying that Anne – the one who wasn't so smart – is Niillas's loved one:

> Anne got the most handsome man of the *siida*
> by trickery,
> voya voya nana nana
> the best in our *siida*,
> voya voya nana nana
> woe, that he would take another person's loved one,
> voya voya nana nana,
> woe, that he would cause Máhtte such sorrow.

47

Niillas grew afraid that he wouldn't get Elle. Máhtte also loved Elle, and she had promised she would be his, which he believed; therefore, he also often made yoiks for Elle:

> Voya voya nana nana,
> this fair girl, the beautiful one,
> she is quick and smart,
> voya voya nana nana,
> pretty and quick,
> the finest in our *siida*.

When Máhtte heard that Niillas had given Elle courting gifts, he made a yoik for her and cried:

> Voya voya nana nana,
> how false she is!

He cried and grieved so much that he almost lost his mind, and he began to hate Niillas and stole reindeer from him. When he got drunk, he cursed and yoiked:

> Voya voya nana nana,
> hell and damnation,
> I'll slaughter Niillas's draft reindeer,
> voya voya nana nana,
> and Elle, the false, damned slut!
> There are too many of that sort,
> voya voya nana nana.

And then he cried some more and kept yoiking. But then Máhtte thought to himself, "It's stupid of me to get mad at Niillas and Elle.

I will probably find an equally nice girl, perhaps an even better one!" Inger, Máhtte's sister, told him, "No one is courting Márjá Andersdatter. She's a good girl, and she's going to be rich, too." Inger was a young and wise woman, and Máhtte said to her, "Do you think Márja would want me?" Inger answered, "I don't know, but I could of course ask Márjá if she would be interested in having you as a husband." And Máhtte liked his sister so much for helping him with courting.

One Sunday Inger went to the *siida* of which Márjá was a member. There she met Márjá and asked her, "Would you like to marry my brother?"

Márjá answered, "Máhtte probably wants no one else but Elle, who is so nice."

"No, I don't think it's that way, believe me when I say that. You two are made for each other," Inger said.

Márjá says, "How can you know that we are made for each other?"

"I have dreamt it, and things usually turn out just the way I dream them," Inger answers.

Then Márjá says, "If that's the way it is, you two may come back in a week. I will think about it until then."

And so they parted ways, and Inger went home. She went to Máhtte and told him what she had heard. Inger and Máhtte's parents were happy to hear the news.

When a week had passed, they went to Márjá's. There is an old tradition among the Sami that, when a young man goes on a courting expedition, the young woman he is courting will meet him and unharness his draft reindeer, as a sign that she wants him. If she doesn't come forward to unharness the suitor's reindeer, he contin-ues driving around the tent and between the tent and the chopping block. If she doesn't come out then, either, he knows that she doesn't want him. The suitor doesn't walk into the tent then but goes straight home. Márjá was aware of all this and knew how she should behave, so when she saw him coming, she went out and unharnessed Máhtte's reindeer. Máhtte then entered the tent and greeted her in the traditional Sami way. The Sami greet each other by putting their arms around each other's necks and pressing their noses together. Máhtte did this, too, and he kissed and hugged Márjá as though he couldn't stop. Then they started to talk and had a few sips of brandy, but there was no coffee to be had at that time. And they married the same day, after which Máhtte wanted to leave for home. Márjá's father, Andaras, asked his daughter to go and get his finest draft reindeer and give it to Máhtte. When Márjá had fetched the reindeer, Máhtte prepared to leave, and Márjá sat down in the sleigh. When they were about to say good-bye, Máhtte and Márjá again put their arms around each other's necks and kissed and hugged, and then they thought there was nothing more they had to do. But then the old man, Andaras, says, "You'll have to make one more trip before you're done. You have to go to the church father and ask for his permission to marry." Máhtte then says, "Does Márjá have another father, or does she have another husband, or how is it?" Máhtte didn't know that the minister had to give his permission, or, as we say now, perform a marriage.

Máhtte was again ready to leave, but now he was afraid that the minister would take his wife. He was almost completely beside himself. It happens sometimes that people get all confused – especially those who are so inclined – when they are planning to get married.

When Máhtte went to Márjá's for a second time, he drove the reindeer he had received from Márjá earlier. They greeted each other in the same manner as before. And those who were in the tent had some drinks and began to talk about the young couple, what they had to do now, and the trip they had to undertake to the minister

the following day. Máhtte worried about losing Márjá to this
minister. He didn't feel like making the trip at all. But Márjá's father
told him that he had to go.

So they prepared themselves for the trip. They brought three
extra draft reindeer and sleighs loaded with meat and reindeer milk.
Andaras, the father, took the three extra reindeer with him, and
Márjá and Máhtte went separately. They had traded reindeer for
ones that were as white as snow and whose harnesses were trimmed
with cloth of many colors. They set off, their reindeer galloping so
fast that the snow blows so hard into the eyes and mouths of those
who are sitting in the sleigh, they can hardly see or breathe. But
when the reindeer have run for a while, they slow down a little and
trot along more calmly. Then it is pleasant to ride and the passengers
begin to yoik:

> Voya voya nana nana nana
> we have real reindeer trotting here,
> voya voya nana nana
> they move like the wind
> voya voya nana nana
> they run straight ahead like a bullet,
> voya voya nana nana
> these reindeer have the biggest antlers of the herd
> voya voya nana nana.

Now the draft reindeer began to get warm and thirsty, and they
snatched some snow to quench their thirst and cool off. Máhtte
pulled in his reindeer, and they all stopped to let their animals rest,
because they had come to the place where they usually let the
reindeer eat snow and relieve themselves. When Inger saw the
reindeer stand and rest, she began to yoik:

The young couple, we wish them happiness
voya voya nana nana
the two young ones will be rich
voya voya nana nana
they will have beautiful children
voya voya nana nana
The beautiful Márjá shines like a light
voya voya nana nana
Then we start up again,
the reindeer begin to trot
voya voya nana nana

And they covered considerable distance; traveled down a steep mountain slope, across a large lake, and up a steep hill. There they had come to another place where the Sami often stopped to let their reindeer rest, and to have themselves a nip. They also used to give a little wine to the guardians of nature, saying, "You shall also have some of my wedding wine!" and pouring some wine on the ground. The person who didn't do this would experience something unpleasant. It was at this spot that a yoik would be sung for the guardians of nature:

You, delicate and beautiful daughters of the earth's guardian
voya voya nana nana
we thank you for having been so good
and for protecting our draft reindeer
from falling down the steep hillside
voya voya nana nana
Thank you, our dear Earth Spirits who protect us
voya voya nana nana
keep protecting our reindeer

voya voya nana nana
our reindeer.

Then they move on. Máhtte put Márjá's reindeer in front of the sleigh. They rode until they came to a trail from another *siida*, and there several reindeer drivers came toward them. Niillas and Elle were among them. They weren't married yet. They kept riding a while until it began to grow dark. Then they stopped to make a fire. They tied the reindeer by their reins to some trees so they could graze.

They boiled some meat, ate, and spent the night there.

When there was daylight again, they packed the sleighs and harnessed the draft reindeer. When the reindeer were ready, the women began to yoik, as it is the habit among the Sami that the women yoik when it is time to set off on a journey. This is what they yoiked:

Voya voya nana nana
here the best draft reindeer of these parts set off
like a flock of birds
Voya voya nana nana
when the long-legged, slender ones leave,
you only see a cloud of snow behind them
Voya voya nana nana
and they float away like the water in the swiftest stream
Voya voya nana nana.

They drove off. When the reindeer noticed that there were people sitting in the sleighs, they started trotting, and they ran like a flock of birds. The trail was nice and flat, so everyone could remain in the sleighs. When they approached the place where the church was located, Márkan, they stopped and waited until everyone had gathered. Then they found lodging in the little cabins and turf huts that were there, and some put up tents.

The next morning, Máhtte and Márjá went to the minister. Again, Máhtte became afraid that the minister would take Márjá away from him. The minister read the text that Máhtte was supposed to repeat: "I take Márjá as my wedded wife and will love and honor her, for better or for worse." "The hell I give you Márjá!" Máhtte swore. "She is my wife, she has been given to me in marriage by Andaras." And he began to tug at Márjá, wanting her to leave with him. But Márjá was sensible and knew what it was all about, so she didn't go along. Then Máhtte, believing that she had forsaken him, walked out. The minister had to end the wedding ceremony, and he called to Máhtte, "It's you that will have Márjá, not I." He realized that Máhtte had misunderstood the whole thing. Márjá then had to teach Máhtte the wedding ceremony and what he was supposed to answer. She knew how to read and had learned the liturgy for weddings. And the next day the minister could complete the ceremony.

When they were finished in church, they went to the cabins and huts and began to celebrate. They only had meat, reindeer milk and liquor. Those who wished to drink did so, and everyone present began to yoik. The young men put their arms around the girls' necks and sang, and some of them cried:

Voya voya nana nana
Oh, you, my love
you are so fair, you are so fine.

And the girls answered:

Voya voya nana nana,
what a man, so fine
so handsome to look at,
voya voya nana nana
you run like the reindeer
you soar like the bird
voya voya nana nana.

And that whole night no one slept.

Niillas hadn't dared to marry before Máhtte was properly married. And it wasn't possible to marry that year, because the Sami had Sabbath with church services only once a year. But they moved together and lived as man and wife.

When the Sabbath came the following year, Niillas and Elle went to Márkan to get married, and all their friends came along. And they held a wedding feast with much eating and drinking. A lot of people came, because Niillas had many relatives and friends. Some of the young men were somewhat resentful because Niillas had gotten Elle, and a young woman named Anne had thought that Niillas had wanted her. But when she understood that Niillas didn't want her, she begun to spread all kinds of rumors about Niillas, including the rumor that he had slept with her. This she told Elle, too. But Elle just said, "It was good of you to give Niillas what he wanted. I can pay you for it." That put a stop to Anne's talking. But people sometimes teased her, saying, "How much did Elle pay you for your help?"

During the wedding dinner, the young couple was supposed to sit at the table, and they were expected to sit there for as long as the wedding party lasted. Some people became drunk during the party and began to yoik:

Voya voya voya nana nana nana
now we're celebrating a wedding
the richest son of the *siida*
has had to submit
Voya voya voya nana nana nana
and to that we drink
voya voya nana nana
the beautiful Elle shines
like the stars in the sky
voya voya nana nana
and now she will move away from us
who will now be the the star of our *siida*?
voya voya nana nana
Now I wish her good luck
voya voya nana nana.

Then it was time for the guests to give the couple wedding presents. They gave money, gold, and reindeer. A person who was honest and had a good memory had been selected to oversee the wedding. He was supposed to remember how much everyone had given and who had promised gifts of reindeer. It was the custom to not accept too much from anyone, because drunk people can give beyond their means. The couple then thanked everyone who had given them presents and wished each giver good fortune.

From Muitalus sámiid birra, *1910*
Translated by Roland Thorstensson

Anders Larsen

The Day Is Dawning

Anders Larsen (1870–1949) is perhaps better known as a newspaper publisher than as a writer of fiction, but he is the author of two short books, both of which are full of material on Sami traditional beliefs, customs, and ways of life during the latter part of the last century and the beginning of the 1900s. Larsen was trained as a teacher and taught in Finnmark while the Norwegianization process was at its most extreme. Because of his involvement in Sami politics, he came into conflict with the Norwegian school authorities. Among other things, he used his newspaper to campaign for the election of Isak Saba, a friend from student years, as the first Sami representative to the Norwegian national parliament. Saba was elected, but Larsen eventually had to leave Finnmark because of his opposition to the assimilation policy. When his paper went bankrupt, he published a novel with the optimistic title *Beaivi-álgu* [Daybreak].

$\mathcal{I}$T WAS A BEAUTIFUL FALL EVENING. Eira sat at the edge of the woods, leaning forward on his hands. A fishing line and hook and a book in Sami lay beside him. He was on his way to the river to catch some small fish and had sat down by an old tree stump and become absorbed in thought.

He had sat like that for a long time and forgotten both fishing and reading. The mild fall evening was so glorious that he just remained sitting there, looking around.

He was at the edge of a little mountain plateau. On both sides of him rose the steep mountains. From the ridge the sharp mountain peaks stood silhouetted against the sky like handsomely branched antlers. Here and there on the peaks there were patches of snow that the summer sun hadn't had time to melt. Further down the mountainside lay the scree, like a grayish shedding from the mountain, and farthest down began the grassland and birch tree woods. Between the two mountains, at the bottom of the short valley, a lake shone like mica, or "crow's silver", as people called it. It wasn't without good reason that the Sami called it Shiny Lake in the old days. Small streams flowed like silver ribbons down the side of the mountain and into the lake, and by the edge of the water, a herd of reindeer was grazing. The evening sun gilded everything and made it beautiful.

The quiet lake at the bottom of the valley embraced it all. It was a large mirror in which everything could be seen upside down; the shore was mirrored at the lake's farthest point, the mountain peaks and the dark blue sky at the lake's nearest point. It was so magnificent that the most talented artist could never create anything like it. It had the same colors as the mountain, the sky, and the forest. And everything was so remarkably clear. And there was life in the picture, as well. Reflections of moving reindeer could be seen in the lake. Only now and then did a fish leap and disturb the splendidly serene picture.

This glorious evening made him melancholy, for he sat in a place marked with memories. He remembered events from bygone days, one after the other. They formed a long and endless series of happy and sad childhood memories. Sometimes he felt such joy that he almost sang, then he abruptly turned so sad that he was almost overcome by tears.

He was sitting at the very place where he had frolicked as a child, picking forget-me-nots and decorating his little sisters and himself with them.

It was exactly at this spot, he said to himself and nodded.

But he also remembered how he, as a child, had lain in the woods, reading the Norwegian catechism over and over, many times, until he began to cry. It was all too difficult and foreign to learn.

But one event, in particular, had become etched on his memory, something which had had great significance for him.

After he had been confirmed, he once heard a boy from a family of reindeer herders read Biblical stories in the Sami language, and that was the first time he realized how helpless he was, because he couldn't really understand one word of Sami, his own language. Never before had he felt so incapable. He was deeply ashamed of himself. The reindeer herding boy's Bible reading echoed in his ears for a long time afterwards.

But he promised himself that he would learn Sami at any cost. It became a matter of conscience for him.

He began buying books written in the Sami language. He studied them intently and tirelessly, day and night, like a person on the verge of losing his sense of time and place. And he eventually learned, but he was not satisfied. It was as if he constantly heard his soul's painful complaint: "You do know how to read Sami, but you don't know how to write in Sami."

He found no peace.

Painstakingly, he set out to learn to write Sami. He ordered books in Sami. He hardly found enough time to sleep. He would get so tired that he fell asleep, only to wake up abruptly, pen in hand. In the end, he learned. But did he ever struggle!

He was very happy when he had learned to both read and write his ancestral language. He felt as if he had conquered the world!

And his love for his mother tongue only increased. He began thinking that there should be schools where every Sami could readily learn to read and write his or her mother tongue.

He recalled, as he was sitting there, how the smug Norwegian boys had laughed at him when he had tried to speak Norwegian as a child. Sometimes he became angry. "You say something in Sami. Then you'll see how it is," he would fling back at them.

And his thoughts wandered far away into the future. In a vision he saw the future of his people. They had acquired status and knowledge and achieved a good way of life for all eternity, so that many Norwegians who knew that they had some Sami blood would speak about it without hesitation; for times had changed so that it had become an honor to be descended from the respected Sami people.

He saw the Sami Canaan before his eyes.

Like Moses of yore, he sat on the top of the mountain and looked out over Canaan, but he himself would not be allowed into this beautiful land.

And while he was sitting there, leaning forward by the old tree stump, it was as if all things around him – the earth, the trees, the rivers and rocks – knew what he was thinking and were friends of the Sami.

His mind kept drifting away, and, half asleep, he felt as if nature around him had come to life and was speaking to him in Sami.

The earth he was lying on spoke to him: "I belong to the Sami. I love you, Sami people. I offer you great riches. I give you what I have, as long as you take care of me. I don't demand that you speak Norwegian. I only ask that you care for me and protect me."

But a young woman, dressed in white, comes walking from the shore, waving a white kerchief. Maria Evje. Smiling, she walks up to Eira. So warm and beautiful. She extends her hand to him, "Nice to see you, Eira!" she says in Sami. Eira, his heart pounding, takes her hand. He is about to answer, but then some ptarmigans cackle and he wakes up.

He is back in somber reality.

Was it only a dream? Will I only be allowed to long and to make wishes that will never be fulfilled, he thought.

Overcome by sadness, he remembers the love he has experienced. Gradually he has forgotten the name Løvgaard. He only thinks of him as a Norwegian rival who once came in his way. And he becomes filled with anger toward all Norwegians. He examines carefully the Norwegians' sins against the Sami, and his ill feelings toward them grow.

And ideas and goals begin to germinate and grow: Like a loyal watchdog, he will respect and watch over the spiritual legacy from his ancestors. He will reprimand each boy and reproach each girl who doesn't cherish the Sami language and who shows no interest in learning to read and write their mother tongue.

It was a nice summer evening in the month of July.

Eira was walking in the hardwood forest above the Sami shopkeeper's home. He had come to this fjord the previous day and had been well received by the shopkeeper. He had sincerely thanked his God for that. So many times he had felt all alone, as if God and human beings had turned their backs on him. Yesterday he had announced that he wanted to talk to the Sami people at the shopkeeper's home. Now he was walking around, thinking about what he would say.

He remembered something that had happened during a trip. The day before he came to this fjord, he had asked a young Sami to row him across the river. At first he spoke Norwegian with this man.

"How much would you like for rowing me across?" he had asked.

The Sami stared at him. He noticed that he was carrying a coat over his arm and assumed he was a well-situated person and a

Norwegian. So he was probably thinking that he could ask for a good deal of money from this man.

"Oh, I should have a crown, I guess."

When they came to the boat, Eira began to speak Sami with the ferry-man. He told him who he was.

They rowed across, and Eira was about to pay his fare. Then the Sami boy said, "I can't take more than 25 øre. I thought you were a Norwegian."

A sense of family probably forbade this money-minded Sami to be greedy.

After dinner a lot of Sami had gathered at the shopkeeper's home. The yard was almost black with people. It was quite a group: old people with faces that were marked by cold and grime and sorrow. People in their best years. An old woman who had stuck a hymn book under her coat: "One doesn't come to a gathering without a book."

Bareheaded, Eira stood by the door of the house and spoke in a loud voice. He explained to his own people what the Sami had been, what they were now, what they ought to be and could be, and what they were going to become.

His voice resounded, "Unite, Sami brothers and sisters! As long as we are divided, we are weak. When we join together, we are strong. Let us love being Sami and show our love with greater passion! Let us stand firmly by the spiritual legacy of our ancestors! Let us never disrespect the Sami name. We have the same rights to the good things in life as any other people. They say that we are an incapable people. So be it! Don't the folk tales tell us that it is the scorned, youngest son who will have the princess and half the kingdom when he uses his strength and vitality to the utmost?"

These forceful words gave new life to his listeners and chased away their anxiety and feelings of inferiority. They straightened their shoulders and began to listen attentively, with mouths agape. These were new words.

"Yes, he sure said it right," they commented to each other.

When Eira had finished, there was wild clapping of hands. Everybody clapped. Those who had come to listen pressed forward to greet and thank him.

"Come and visit me sometime," many said.

When the Sami returned to their homes, it was as if their eyes had been opened. Now they had heard what the Sami people had been, what they were now, and what they were going to be. They thought it was as though the light of dawn had begun to shine.

It was as if a new day had begun for them.

From Beaivi-álgu, *1912*
Translated by Roland Thorstensson

Matti Aikio

Rafting Down the Tana River

Matti Aikio (1872–1929) was a Sami from Kárášjohka/Karasjok in Finnmark, Norway, the heart of Sapmi. His mother tongue was Sami, but he nonetheless preferred to write his books in Norwegian. He is unquestionably the first professional Sami writer, and his books were, in fact, both noticed and discussed by the national media in Norway. Aikio moved to Oslo, where he quickly became a legendary figure in the capital city's artist colony. Because of his condescending attitudes toward the coastal Sami in particular, he was not embraced wholeheartedly by more progressive Sami for quite some time. Aikio's entire authorship revolves around the problems of mixed cultures and a person's identity. These are timely topics, which should make his writings appeal to today's multicultural readers.

OUT IN THE FIELDS, women and small boys rake the rubbish together and haul it away with wheelbarrows; they smash the chunks of dung with long-handled clubs and spread it over the soil with rakes. That is farming, too. Erki Lemik Issak is the only one this far up the country who has a cart, a work cart he made himself; he has even spliced the steel bands around the wheels, something that several besides himself are proud of. And since Olle is his good neighbor, he gets to borrow the cart to haul away the piles of rubbish, and to use it for a few other chores as well. No, there are no roads for summer driving here. What purpose does a cart really have? The river is used for boat travel, and animal trails across the tundra are used to deliver the mail.

The horses roam freely across the land now; they have not moved up into the high country yet. And the stallions fight over the mares; not only boys, but adults too, take sides for this or that stallion. Recently Olle was hit and kicked by another, older boy, Marja Piera, when the big, red stallion that Olle's father, Ville Jongo, had purchased in Finland last year emerged victorious from a fight with a stallion belonging to Marja Piera's uncle and castigated the other horse so thoroughly that it had to circle around, dejected, at a respectful distance. Oh, how humiliating for Marja Piera and his side!

It was not with any particular enthusiasm that Olle, together with a half-grown sister, labored in the field with the manuring, not because he was lazy, for he was strong as steel, but because this was an insignificant job for a man. And the boys in the other houses, where there were enough women, usually did not have to work with manuring. His father, Ville Jongo, worked in the smithy or at his carpenter's bench all day, and Olle's older brother was logging together with grown-ups.

Today Ville Jongo had started sawing a large log into thin boards used for building river boats. The log had been rolled up on a high platform on the lower side of a small slope, below the wood cutting area. Jongo and his farm hand stood at either end of the peeled log and were in the process of snapping saw lines with a string blackened with a mixture of soot and water. Ville lifted the tight string and let it snap, and the black line was in place. They used a plumb line at the ends and marked the bottom, turned the log over and snapped saw lines on the other side, too. Then they started sawing with the long, wide saw. Ville himself stood on top of the platform, the farm hand below. They began at the root end and sawed a couple of handbreadths in, then Ville hammered a wedge into the kerf, and now the sawing went like a dance.

The sawing could be heard from the sandy banks of the river, too. There, people were busy disassembling the small log cabins they had built during the spring and tying them into rafts. Halle Johanas had boards and a few dozen round logs to take along as well.

Every evening Olle and the other boys went down to the river to watch and help. Halle Johanas's raft consisted of three sections securely tied between long, straight birch trunks by means of ties made of small, thin, twisted birches. The outer edge of the raft had a kind of timber frame railing that was rather low, used for the four-fathoms-long timber oars with which the raft was to be steered.

Two or three such smaller rafts were then tied together with birch trunks, one raft after the other.

Some of the rafts had come all the way from that valley where villager Sire Andaras had established his reindeer camp last winter, and they had already been tested in the river's rapids up there.

A raft comes swinging around the river's bend, over on the other side. It is Andi Piera's raft. Andi Piera, the miracle with property, even though he was not married yet, and a real scatter-brain, because he could not get Elle to stay in his bedroom.

Anda Juoksa, who lived on the slope by the church, also stood here on the bank of the river.

"When a bachelor gets his house ready in the way Andi Piera does," he said. "Only a subterranean girl will become a wife in a house like that."

These were just words that Anda Juoksa let slip, they were not at all based on what people thought. But such demonic words stick in people's minds. God damn Anda Juoksa! It was like putting a curse on Anda Piera. Now everyone would repeat what Anda Juoksa had said. People like Anda Juoksa deserved to be hanged.

71

Old Anarasj-Marja from Enari, who for some reason or another had been sentenced by fate to walk bent over at a very sharp angle, with her round corner pointing skyward, comes up along the bank breathing hard, with her face low down like that of an animal. She wanted to know if people needed more rope. Because it was Anarasj-Marja who twisted the ropes, combining the long, thin runners of the pine roots with the fiber in the Russian flour bags. She was practically the only one doing that job here. Every winter she drove from Enari in Finland to this area, always lodged with Erki Lemik Issak, and soon started twisting ropes from fiber and root runners. And she always had her sled full of dried fish from Enari Lake. The slightest suggestion of teasing from the little boys made her mad as an irritated lemming – oh Lord, how the upturned face that was so close to the ground, how that face at the end of the down-hanging torso could rave. It raved in a broken mix of Norwegian and Sami. No one understood her peculiar Sami dialect from Enari.

At the last minute, Anarasj-Marja still managed to sell some rope. Greedy until death she was, with her skin shoes full of silver coins.

All the stuff sacks and food bags were brought on board the boats. Juhas Juhasj had a cow on his raft, too, a dowry for a daughter who had gotten married last winter to a man down by the coast.

Andijn was on board Halle Johanas's raft, and Hoock and his wife, too; they wanted to accompany their daughter down river for awhile. There were no less than five or six rafts that were now pushed off from the shore and started drifting around the village on the spit. Wives and girls and others remained on the banks both up and down the river, calling out:

"Farewell! Farewell!"

A great moment once again! And on board there were shots of liquor for the leave-taking. There was always someone who wanted to come along for awhile. The spring flood was wonderfully large, and the current twice as strong as when the water was at its normal level during the summer.

A couple of spits below the village, Hoock and his wife were rowed ashore, while the rafts continued drifting downriver undisturbed.

Andijn stood on the raft and waved, and she felt the lack of mercy in the situation: to be carried on a log raft downriver by an overpowering spring flood.

Those who had rowed the visitors ashore came rowing behind.

Halle Johanas made a fire on his raft, on top of a piece of turf that he had brought along for that purpose, and hung the coffee pot above it, asking Andijn to keep an eye on it. He and his partner normally had to stand at opposite ends of the long raft in order to steer it with the long wooden oars, so that the raft stayed in the middle of the current.

Some of the rafts were still close enough for people to call to each other.

They passed one river spit after another. All the sandbanks and outlying hay fields on the lower parts of the river spits had disappeared under water; flocks of ducks swam inside the thickets of birch and willow. It was almost midnight. It was absolutely calm. On the south side, the slopes of pine were covered by sunlight, and they shone golden and light green, and the curlicues of river whirls proved refreshing to Andijn's spirit. The otherwise so calm river was now moving powerfully. Pieces of washed-out river bank proved it, too. The rejoicing tones of a thrush burst forth this morning, then died away in the distance behind, and from that which approached, new tones flowed out, filling the valley this sunlit night.

A couple of miles below the village, the river merged with another river that came from the south, delineating the border with Finland.

Now it really was like drifting down a big river.

"There's Suomi-Finland," Halle Johanas said to Andijn.

"Yes, I know, I have often traveled here in the winter time."

How strangely barren it was on the south shore, the Finnish side. The mountain, actually quite high to be a mountain in this part of the country, rose steeply from the flat strips of land between the river and the foot of the mountain.

Here, the pine forest also started disappearing, mostly on the Finnish side, the southwestern shore.

Tiny villages consisting of a couple of small houses were seen every now and then, but initially only on the Finnish side. A mile below the confluence of the two rivers, small, solitary villages began appearing on the Norwegian side as well.

By Borjas-njarga, Sail Spit, a village on the Norwegian side, a few small stretches of white water began. Andijn found them exhilarating and invigorating, the waves washing over the raft a little bit, the refreshing thrill of the speed of the raft down such fast water.

"That's Outakoski on the Finnish side," said Halle Johanas, "What you see is the new school building."

"Yes, I have been there too," Andijn replied.

In the morning they passed a small, cozy island, called Suolu, on the Norwegian side six miles below the inland village. Here the river began moving almost straight, flowing steadily. The wind started to blow, and it got cloudy and cold. The mountains became higher and more barren on the Norwegian side, too. Everything suddenly became kind of desolate and gloomy. On the Finnish side, the steep mountain, richly covered with reindeer moss, dove almost straight down into the river.

A feeling of dejection comes over Andijn, and she lies down on top of a couple of stuff sacks and pulls a blanket over herself, but she still freezes. The world has once again become so desolate and lonely. Andijn cries; tired and sleepy that she is, it is difficult for her to collect her thoughts. In a way, everything is indifferent to her now, because whatever her thoughts touch is melancholy. She falls asleep, and Halle Johanas comes over and throws some additional clothing on top of her.

The weather turned stormy, and the rafts had to pull ashore to avoid drifting onto some inhospitable stretch of the shore.

Towards afternoon it calmed down, and the rafts were steered out into mid-channel again.

In the evening, eight miles from the upland village, the current gained a threatening speed. Halle Johanas and his friend ran back and forth on the raft, tying down every loose thing with ropes. Andijn's heart pounded.

"Couldn't I be rowed ashore here?"

"No, that's not necessary here," Halle Johanas called back.

A small inn could be seen up on a steep slope on the northern, Norwegian side, and, to the north, a great glacier was visible, a halo of sunlight around its cap of snow and ice.

Far below, something roared and rumbled like subterranean thunder.

"For God's sake, put me ashore!" Andijn cried.

"It is too late now," Halle Johanas called, and Andijn also saw that it was too late. And before she knew it, the first waves washed in over the raft. She ran forward and desperately clung onto Halle Johanas's jacket.

"Don't grab me!" Unmercifully he pushed her away and, his teeth clenched, he steered the raft through the churning masses of water in this long stretch of rapids that filled the air with a deafening roar. Andijn lay there, holding her hands over her eyes. The waters washed in over the raft again and again, and each time Andijn called out and gasped for air like one who is drowning. This stretch of the river was full of great boulders that stuck up during low water; but now they were covered and created powerful whirls that spewed out white. Even the shores were covered with great boulders thrown all over. But Halle Johanas and all the other rafters were used to traveling on white water since childhood, and could see the worst dangers far away and steer their rafts to avoid them.

The raft gained some extra speed, and then the water got calm again. It had not taken more than a few minutes to travel down these long rapids.

But the river continued to hurry from one rapid to another. With few exceptions, it would do that for the next eight miles.

The valley had become narrow down here. Only occasionally did it widen to make room for a few small homesteads nestled in birch forest.

Andijn walks up to the bow of the raft again and says to Halle Johanas, "Now that it's over, it seems it was almost fun."

"That was just child's play, wait until we float down the Wolf's Gap."

"You'll put me ashore there, right?"

"Of course."

"But is it dangerous to stay on the raft?"

"It depends on how you look at it. It is definitely not without danger."

Andijn remains silent. Then she says, "But it would be exciting to try it."

"You have to take responsibility for that decision yourself."

The raft is devoured by one rapid after the other and is sent on its way.

A couple of miles further downstream, Juhas Juhasj, whose raft is now just ahead of Halle Johanas's calls:

"The Otsejok church is up there in that small valley. It's a stone church, and Vir'kal preaches there now; he's a great preacher. People come from far away to listen to him. He preaches what Laestadius taught. And many people around here have gotten the faith since Vir'kal came."

The raft rushes on with the strong current. There is a homestead here, another there, each about a mile apart.

A new roar can be heard far below, a distant, threatening din.

"Shall I row you ashore while there's still time?" Halle Johanas says to Andijn. "That way you can walk across the ridge. Just follow the trail to the end until you get to a homestead below Big Falls; it's the last house on the Finnish side."

Andijn just stands there, unable to make up her mind.

"I think I dare. There's no rush to get ashore yet. I think I dare."

The raft starts floating with greater speed, and the din and the roar grows louder. Andijn is suddenly seized by a helpless, paralyzing fear.

"Row me ashore!"

Halle Johanas turns pale. That was in the last ... minute. He shoves the boat from the platform on the raft.

"Jump into the boat!" And he rows towards the shore with all his strength. "Get out!" The next moment he chases the raft like a madman and reaches it just as it is quickly pushed into the first great whirls of water – gets the boat pulled up onto the raft, but does not have time to tie down the boat's painter to the raft. He ties a rope around his waist and secures it to the platform so he won't be washed overboard, shoves the oar in the water, and steers straight ahead. The Wolf's Gap is squeezed between steep, rocky walls and flat stones so sheer that Halle Johanas sees that just ahead the channel is like a smooth lake. Rocks below the surface throw man-sized, twisted waves up over the masses of water. They are alive like white flames, but are pressed together and carried away by the storm. The cow on Juhas Juhasj's raft bellows with terror, but it cannot be heard; its large, frightened eyes stare ahead; but there is nothing for the animal to do but try to remain standing on its four strong legs and stare at this roaring, boiling abyss. The raft rocks quickly down the river, its bow constantly lifting and diving.

Now! Suddenly this eternity was over and done with in a few minutes. All the rafts save one came through mostly intact, drifting forward in the weak current below the Wolf's Gap. But one of them had been torn apart when it hit a rock below the surface close to the shore on the Finnish side, and Juhas Juhasj said to the people who remained on what was left of it:

"Well, it is damned typical that some people are always tempted to steer too close to the other side. There are always people who don't know; they worry that the raft will come too close to the other shore in that gentle curve. But the waters don't push towards shore there – they follow the curve."

Here, by the Wolf's Gap, the river lost the Finnish border, or, more accurately, the border lost the river and took off across the mountains, first in a southerly direction, then far eastward, and did not meet a real river until it reached the Russian border far to the east, by Grense-Jakobselv.

Below the Wolf's Gap, the river turned into a much calmer spring flood, passing through an idyllic landscape with small farms on either side of the river banks and a small chapel on a flat piece of ground on the south shore.

Not until they had come out of the Wolf's Gap did Halle Johanas have a chance to look back, and he then soon discovered that his boat was gone. His partner, who stood at the stern of the raft and held the steering oar, called to him that the boat had been washed overboard far upstream.

They started looking for the boat on the calmly flowing river. Yes, there it was, drifting downriver, torn up from one side to the other.

"What the hell!" Juhas Juhasj called from his raft, "Is that your boat, Halle Johanas?"

Juhas Juhasj rowed out to retrieve the badly damaged boat and towed it to Halle Johanas's raft. At that time, not much was said about it. The Wolf's Gap sometimes requires an offering.

But the partner swore. Why on earth should Halle Johanas row that damned girl ashore? And when she didn't want to go ashore the first time, they should just have tied a rope around her and attached it to a crossbeam instead.

Halle Johanas was pale and quiet. "But we don't have to tell the others about it," he said. "Let's call the whole thing an accident!"

The rafts pulled ashore on a sandy beach on the north side. It was time to sleep. Morning had come, and the wind had begun to blow a bit – it would become difficult to steer the rafts in the weak current down here.

Lemik Jounas's farmstead was located on the river bank here. Lemik Jounas was a well-to-do bachelor, and everyone expected that he would marry the fabulously beautiful Marja who lived on the south shore. And Marja was not just beautiful, she was also nice and kind and hard-working, and in this part of the country all traveling officials and ministers and lawyers and such gentlemen lodged with Marja and her parents when it was time to halt. But Lemik made no attempts in that direction. He looked like a gentleman himself, fair and tall, and had a long, narrow face. But perhaps he did not appreciate that Marja every now and then had important men for guests. If only she knew. No, first of all, it is difficult to know such things; secondly, very difficult to believe them. Faith and trust are noble but hopelessly rare gifts.

Lemik Jouna asked how people were doing up there in the upland village.

"Just fine," Juhas Juhasj replied, "and, on one of the rafts that's coming, there's a woman you might find interesting, unless she perishes in the Wolf's Gap, of course. I suggest you row out to the raft and take a good look at her! She has mittens with red embroidery on them, and a fur coat and sweater in the chest at home."

A boat arrived from the Finnish side with Andijn on board.

"I don't know how to thank you enough, Johanas, for rowing me ashore at the last minute. I would have died of fright if I had stayed on your raft, I realize that now."

Later, Halle Johanas and his partner sit on the raft, staring at the completely ruined boat. They are both depressed. Now they have to rent a boat when they head upriver again. They have to bring supplies back home when they return from the Midsummer market by the river mouth.

"And last winter you lost your horse, Johanas," his partner says. "That was Andijn's fault, too."

"Let's just stop talking about it right now," Halle Johanas says. But he could not take his eyes off the ruined boat – it was one of Ville Jongo's masterpieces, which Halle Johanas had purchased last year for forty kroner. Forty kroner does not grow on trees in the upland country, and that boat he could have used for many, many years. And the horse he could have used for many, many years. The boat was the new type of river boat that Ville Jongo had designed about ten years ago and for which he had received a medal at an exhibition in Tromsø. It was thirty feet long and only three feet wide at the widest point. In front, the upper sides were spliced with a thicker board that was not bent by force, but cut to shape. This made the front section stronger, and it also had a natural fork for the oarlock. The high stem was stretched forwards and had a small bow grip that was curved in and carved, about as wide as the width of a hand and facing the length of the boat. The bow was somewhat wide on top, so that the boat was lifted up when punted upstream across the stretches of rapids. The sternpost was lower.

No, Halle Johanas could not take his eyes off the boat. Now he looked at it because it was wrecked. Before he had often looked at it because all its marvelously beautiful lines would make his mouth water. It was tarred and still shone reddish and light brown.

The rafters, who had barely slept a wink during the trip, slept all day.

Towards evening the wind died, and the rafts were steered into the current again. It was only now that Andijn learned that Halle Johanas's boat had been wrecked during the passage through the Wolf's Gap, and she was very unhappy about it. But she did not realize that she was responsible for it. And Halle Johanas remained silent about the whole thing. But his partner could not keep quiet any longer.

"Johanas did not have time to tie the boat to the raft when he came rowing back. He should have put you ashore much earlier."

A shadow crossed Andijn's face.

"In that case I want to pay for the boat."

"What he says is just a bunch of rubbish," Halle Johanas said, his voice trembling.

"I would like to know if it is my fault."

"It is not your fault, and let's not talk about it any more."

And Andijn remained silent. She remembered that she had been responsible for the death of his horse last winter and that her father had not wanted to reimburse Johanas for it. It all felt so vague and icy in her mind, where it lingered for a long, long time. She froze, she got hot, and she froze again, until she eventually became obsessed with the thing that held the fever: the realization that she had no idea of where this drifting would lead. Should she go to that town in the east, where Einar Asper lived, or should she continue down to the river mouth, where the district judge lived, and where her aunt also lived. Oh God, if she could only go far, far away with a ship! But, of course, one cannot do that, and the world out there does not care much about one's sorrows. They are just chaff in the hard, hard world.

Well below the Wolf's Gap, the river turned northward. A couple of miles downstream, a single rapid was passed – the last one – and here they came upon the province's first main road. It crossed a low, two-mile-wide isthmus on the east shore, continuing on eastward along the north shore of the long fjord to the few towns and fishing villages located there.

On the river bank at the very end of the road stood the young and friendly Jao Jao, a half-Finn, who had recently started a small business in a shed, which he called "The Mustard Seed."

"How's 'The Mustard Seed' going, Jao Jao?" Juhas Juhasj called from his raft.

"Excellent, Juhas Juhasj! Soon I will have to add on to my storage buildings, but I won't start eating and drinking, like the merchant in the Scripture, and then the Lord will also protect me from dying tomorrow."

"Yes, he is wise who plants a mustard seed at the end of a new main road."

The birch forests on the slopes on both sides looked like they were ailing here. The river became wider, and to the far north the naked blue mountains could already be seen on either side of the river mouth.

Andijn runs to the front of the raft, to Halle Johanas.

"Put me ashore, Johanas! I want to go to town."

"But we have no boat we can use now. You should have said that earlier, then we could have called to Jao Jao and asked him to get you."

Andijn remains silent. Then she says, "Well, in a way it's better that it's too late. When it comes down to it, I'd rather go to the river mouth, to my aunt."

And Andijn returns to the stern.

It is far between the steep, upright mountains on both sides of the river mouth. The huge, sandy beaches are covered by the spring flood; there are wide, completely flat areas with birch forest and a small farm here and there on either side. The mountain to the west is just a pile of rocks. The one to the east shines of red sand stone and violet rock faces in the midnight sun.

The fjord is blue between steep, golden mountains.

From Bygden på elveneset, *1929*
Translated by Lars Nordström

Hans Aslak Guttorm

Winter Night

Hans Aslak Guttorm (1906–1992) is in many ways the link between the Sami writers of the first part of the twentieth century and the generation of writers that appeared on the literary scene in the 1960s and 1970s. Guttorm went to Jyväskylä in southern Finland in the 1930s with the intention of becoming a teacher, and he wrote several manuscripts in Sami during his years as a student there. Only one manuscript was published during that time, *Koccam spalli* [Rising Wind], which appeared in 1940, the same year as the outbreak of WWII. The other manuscripts remained in his desk drawer until the the first Sami-owned and Sami-managed publishing company released them as a series of monographs in the 1980s. Significantly, it was Guttorm who was honored by being nominated as the first Sami candidate for the Nordic Prize for Literature in 1984; nominated for work which had existed only in manuscript form for close to fifty years.

*J*T WAS ALREADY GETTING DARK. Woodchopper-Sammul was in full swing at the chopping block. The chips flew as his axe struck the frozen wood, and the sound carried far into the distance. Next to the logs that had been stacked upright lay a load which Sammul had just hauled down from the mountains with his ox. The harness was still fastened between the shafts of the sled. The ox was pacing around on the hard-packed snow in the farmyard, the frosty snow crunching beneath its hoofs. Veiled in the smoky steam that flowed out through the half-opened door of the barn, the ox lowed now and then. Between the blows of his axe, Sammul could hear the sounds of his wife doing chores. The door to the shed creaked, and the barn door groaned as Máret, Sammul's wife, shouldered her way into the barn with a load of hay. The smoke rose above the trees like a pillar, only slightly bent by the biting northerly wind. From the mountain one could hear lichen gatherers yelling commands to their horse. In the north the sky glowed red, and along the horizon it was edged in ice-blue light. This was the period of Arctic twilight, when the sun has grown tired and set, leaving behind two months of winter sky.

At dawn the moon had finished its climb up Áitevárri. Its light was reflected on the frost-covered tree trunks. The morning star shone amidst the myriad of stars in the southeast, twinkling down on Geavuvuopmi lying asleep under the heavy, cold winter cover. Sammul was chopping wood, stopping only now and then to listen and look. In the house he heard his boy cry, their only child.

Down the hill, on the trail they used when gathering lichens, Sammul's brother, Niilas, came running with a load of ptarmigans, dashed past the chopping block on his way toward the main road, and disappeared behind the scrub. Sammul thought he heard something or other from further down. On Stallonjunni, on the Norwegian side, sounds rose occasionally above a steady drone. Sammul held his breath and listened. Then he turned around and went into the house.

Máret stood by the hot stove, cooking. She still had her barn coat on, and the boy was sitting in the bed, shaking a tobacco box he had been given to play with. When Sammul had taken a long time to warm up, he finally broke his silence with: "Brrr, it sure is frigid out there. Even my toes are cold."

Máret glanced quickly at his fur boots and said, "But why haven't you put anything warmer on your feet?"

Sammul answered, "Well… these boots ought to be good enough for here at home. I'll use the others when I go out to set up traps."

Sammul put some logs on the fire, and Máret stirred the soup. Sammul said, "I heard some noise down below when I was out."

"Really… well, they'll probably start moving over on the Norwegian side soon. The mailman said yesterday, remember, that Widower-Máhtte's herd is on its way up from the lowlands just under Gáissaguolban. That's probably what you heard."

Sammul put on his fur mittens again and went out onto the steps. From there he could see above the scrub and far down along the Geavu river. He could make out sounds of dogs barking, reindeer grunting, bells clanging, and people yelling. The sounds came together and formed one big roar in the sea of steaming frost. Through this roar he could hear yoiking: "As the frost smoke rises to the sky…." Then he couldn't distinguish some of the words, but he heard the end clearly: "Widower-Máhtte's herd is racing on…."

He first caught sight of the herd as it was coming across Stuollo-njárga headland, and after a little while he could make it out the way one does a person who is approaching on foot through a heavy snowfall. Sammul could hear Máhtte calling out in a dialect from the western mountains, "Hey, get over there, get along, get! Boy, that one is sure frisky – chasing them around even worse than the wolves."

"That must be Máhtte," Sammul said.

The reindeer at the front of the herd had reached the house. Here Máhtte himself stopped with the lead reindeer. Little by little, the animals came to a halt. Someone with an unharnessed reindeer was driving his sled standing up; only his upper body could be seen as he disappeared into the cascade of snow and steam from the snorting animals. Máhtte's hired man, who was leading the string of reindeer and sleds, stopped and chained the draft reindeer to the corner of the storehouse behind the barn. Máhtte's wife burst forth through the snow, heading for the storehouse. Her child was bundled in the front of the little sleigh, and the dog followed after on a leash.

From behind the barn came the sound of harnesses rattling. Máhtte's hired man, Piera, was busy taking the harnesses off the draft reindeer. Gutnel from the Westland appeared from behind the barn, carrying her baby in a bundle; she walked up to the house.

The door opened. This mountain woman, wrapped in layers of warm clothes, stepped inside and greeted the people in the house.

"I'll put the kid here against the bed while I take off my things. I'm so bundled up, it's like unharnessing an animal."

She took off a couple of reindeer fur coats, loosened three shawls – one was over her coat, two were on her head, one on top of the other. The baby, whom the mother called Sammul, squirmed in the cradle, kicking his legs against the wraps and trying to free his little hands. He stared at the lamp that was hanging from the ceiling. Gutnel hung her clothes up on the pegs between the door to living room and the small room next to it. Then she took a piece of fire wood and scraped the snow off herself before proceeding to nurse the baby.

Piera also came stealing into the house with his bag of traveling provisions, and with him came a rush of cold air. Then pots began to rattle, and the cooking was in full swing.

Outside, several people were standing around, brushing snow off their clothes. Máhtte and the other hired man, Biehtar, slipped into the house. In the rush of the cold air they noticed the smell of pipe smoke.

They greeted those inside.

Máhtte walked up to the stove. He sat down on the woodbox, pulled out his pipe from his shoulder bag, dug up some smoldering tobacco with his knife, and begun to suck.

"It's cold," Máhtte began.

"Yeah, it's been freezing cold for several weeks now. It was… when was it again? Oh, now I remember, last Friday, when I went out to check the traps, it had warmed up a little, but now it's bone-chilling cold again.... Last night the water froze in the bucket, even though we had put it next to the stove," Sammul continued.

"But we've had plenty of light," Máhtte said.

Gutnel and Máret sat at the edge of the bed, each with a baby on her lap. Máret asked for reindeer skin for leggings in exchange for a pair of knitted mittens.

The two hired men sat by the door, putting sedge grass into their shoes. They laid wet shoes and leggings out to dry. They walked around with their fur shoes unlaced, sedge grass hanging out over the tops and all the way down to the floor. It was Biehtar's turn to be with the herd that night.

They talked all evening. Máhtte told them about his summer work, what he had experienced, how he had frightened the wolf.

They sat down to eat. Sammul, his wife, and Ante, their little son, sat at the table, while the family of reindeer herders had their meal around a bench by the stove. The steam rose from the meat trough and hovered like a thick fog in the cold room. They slurped and ate. In the middle of the meal, Máhtte started to think about wolves and asked Sammul, "Any graylegs in the area these days?"

"Well, it wouldn't surprise me if they've already helped themselves to some of the reindeer in your herd. There have been wolves around, that's for sure, both small and large packs. Take that time I was running around checking my cormorant traps. I was at Ávžžijeaggi... there was so much howling one evening, I just about lost my hearing listening to it."

"When was that? Gutnel asked.

"Well, not long ago at all," Sammul answered, pausing and blowing on his spoon.

"Biehtar should probably go out to the herd right away," said Gutnel.

"Should I take the draft reindeer?"

91

"I think it's best to let the reindeer be loose." Gutnel answered. "They're easy prey for the wolves when they're tethered."

Biehtar put on his wraps and went outside, untied the draft reindeer from the stakes and led them to the herd. Their hoofs crackled and his skis creaked as he disappeared into the frosty woods on the Norwegian side of the river.

Gumpečohkka rose at an angle on the Norwegian side. It was a big, barren mountain that towered above all the others. A wolf let out a howl that echoed among the peaks, a sound that cut to the bone. Soon Biehtar heard another and then yet another. The wolves were howling in unison. Their piercing cries traveled like a song of death. A falling star spread its glowing rain over Gumpečohkka's white peak. Northern lights lay in wait above the mountains.

The wolves quieted down, listened a while, then started their long, undulating hungry howling again.

Far away in Gumpegirku, behind Gumpečohkka, the chorus of another pack of wolves could be heard. Their howling echoed back from the mountains on the Finnish side of the river. Máhtte could hear Naste barking at the edge of the herd on Dažavárri.

Máhtte said to Piera, "You probably have to go out to the herd, too, Piera. The wolves are howling something awful out there. Biehtar can't handle it all alone now – I don't even know if he brought his rifle along."

"Is it quiet at Gumpegirku?" Gutnel asked as she laid the baby in the cradle by the stove.

"There's howling everywhere. Even in the sky," said Máhtte as he went outside.

Piera got dressed, put sedge grass into his shoes and fur mittens. Laced up. Stood up, grabbed an old coat that had the fur on the inside, and over it he put a thick coat made of the skin of a reindeer yearling. Then he pulled a cap down over his head, put the lasso over his shoulder and a rifle, an old Russian gun, under his arm. And then he he took off over the crisp snow drifts and disappeared into the Norwegian woods.

The reindeer stood still and listened. Clustered together, they stared in the direction of the wolves' howling. Snow was rolling down the hillside in white balls.

Biehtar yelled,"You stay on the south side of the hill. They'll probably try to get into the herd from that direction!"

Piera bounded toward the steep slope. The reindeer were on their guard, their ears standing straight up. Ready to run. Naste barked and kicked the snow with his hind legs.

Piera yelled, but Biehtar soon made him stop; you could lose your voice if you yelled too loudly at a wolf. They exchanged a few words. The wolves heard them and howled again.

Muste ran along the river and howled, too. They heard Gutnel call to the dog, "Hey, Muste, get away from there so they won't eat you, too!" But Muste was nowhere to be seen, only his baying could be heard through the copse; it reverberated so that the wolves stopped howling for a moment to listen. Muste, too, fell silent and listened to the sound as it traveled from mountain top to mountain top and finally disappeared into eternity. Then he started up again.

Varge had also come down on the ice, barking and stamping his feet. He, too, wanted to take part in scaring the enemy. Angrily he leaped at the sounds over and over again, stopped and howled, and whined when he didn't manage to quiet the wolves down. Varge probably wasn't too keen on getting into a fight with the wolves. Once last summer, he had set off on his own, and then the wolves had snapped at him.

Piera fired his rifle. A long flame shot out toward the sky. Biehtar's rifle went off, too, and the mountains thundered.

93

Muste tired of barking, turned around and slowly walked back to Varge, as if Varge or his partner had called out a warning to not get closer to the wolves. Together they ran back to the house and stood at the door, scraping and whining. The door opened. Taking the cold air with them, Muste and Varge forced themselves inside, panting and puffing. Their tongues hung to the floor. They disappeared under the table to slurp from their bowl of meat broth.

Niilas, Sammul's brother, was coming along Áiteavzi with a load of reindeer lichen, his sled squeaking its way to the stack. At the stack he stopped the horse, a gray mare. It walked around outside for a while before Niilas led it into the stable. Then he unloaded. The sled creaked. Piera and Biehtar could hear it clearly from the hillside at Njiejatanvárri.

The wolves' howling had died down. For a long time, nature's peace reigned. Diamonds shone from the trees. Stars twinkled from the heavenly vault. In the snow, thousands of eyes gleamed back at the sky. The reindeer looked as though they were asleep. The dog had curled up at Biehtar's feet. But its ears were moving. Piera sat at the bottom of Gumpečohkka.

Suddenly Naste began to bark. Biehtar and his companion quickly talked over what to do next. The reindeer got up on their feet and sniffed in the direction of the mountain.

Biehtar fired a shot up toward the peak. Piera shouted. Naste barked and tried to run toward the mountain but had to give up because of the deep snow. The reindeer tried to hide behind each other. Their bells clanked.

Then they heard growling and panting from up above. Biehtar fired. But it didn't do much good. Black shadows leaped out from behind the frosty trees. The reindeer ran in all directions. They kicked up a storm of snow as they fled. The bells clanked, the herders shouted, and Naste barked as if he had gone mad. The herd of reindeer swerved around on the ice of the Geavu river and were pushed toward the Finnish side, the wolves right behind them.

Biehtar and his companion kept firing, but not one of their shots managed to hit its mark. They slipped on their skis and went down the hill, all the way down to the smooth Geavu river, where they stopped. On the Finnish side, shadows were moving. They heard the clanging of the bell of a young female reindeer, and frosty steam drifted by like little clouds. From the woods over on the Finnish side they could hear the gnashing of sharp teeth, the crunching of limbs and the sounds of flesh being ripped to pieces. The wolves had attacked their prey. The two hired men caught sight of three of the predators standing over a carcass, tearing at it. They took aim, the butt of their rifles against their chins. Two blinding flames shot out at the same time, and a cloud of smoke hung in the air in front of them.

They stood there a moment. The smoke lifted, and they ran closer. Two wolves were dead, and one lay kicking in the snow. It exhaled, and the pool of blood under its chest shone red and gradually seeped into the snow. Limbs were strewn all around, and the snow was covered with blood and pieces of fur. It looked like a battlefield.

Their hearts were pounding, almost as though their chests might explode. But from the field they could hear the yearlings grunt and a few bells clang.

Then they set off, following the tracks made by two of the beasts of prey. They goaded the dog to come along. At first Naste wouldn't move. He just stood barking beside the wolf that was shaking in its death throes. But finally he managed to tear himself away. He sniffed in the direction of the riverbank on the Finnish side and bounded away. Biehtar and Piera followed behind and examined the tracks. There was blood in the snow from one of the wolves. The tracks led to a thicket by the river. Naste went ahead of the

95

others, whining with excitement and barking now and then as he waited for the men. The dog was in a hurry. It was easy to move forward on skis, and for Naste it was easy to run in the tracks of the wolves. He looked back now and then, wagged his tail and moved his ears and showed that he was in the mood for a chase. He didn't have the sense to be afraid of the predators. After he had killed a wolf pup up in the high mountains last summer, he felt tough and sure of himself. He wasn't very big, Naste, but ferocious and quite strong.

The wolf tracks led in the direction of the mountain, between Niilas' house and barn, through the gate, and up toward the hill on the trail they used when they gathered lichen. There were still patches of blood here and there in the snow.

Piera was in the lead; he hurried ahead, his skis whistling against the hard packed snow, his pole creaking, and his breathing forming clouds of steam around his face.

Biehtar whispered, "Listen, one of us has to go back to the herd. They can attack it even if it's in the yard, and we can't do much now with the ones that got scared off, anyway."

Biehtar turned his skis and set off in the direction of the herd. He heard Muste barking far away on the winter road. Varge was howling at the far end of the field.

Piera continued on, with Naste in the lead. The tracks led toward the windy open highlands. The lichen road stretched along the middle of the mountain and straight across Roavveaja, and opposite it Naste turned to the right along the ridge, looking back before disappearing behind the frosty scrub and whining as if he wanted to get Piera's attention.

Piera took off one of his coats and followed behind. The wolves had run zigzag through the scrub before coming into the woods where the snow was harder, almost so hard that they didn't break through. Naste followed the tracks and sniffed at patches of blood.

At Vaddaraige the wolves had turned toward Gorsaravda and from there down into a valley. On the hillside there was loose snow. Up on the riverbank, Piera could see how the wolves had gone through the snow, leaving big depressions. He looked up toward Áiteskaidi for tracks. But the moon was already waning and didn't give him enough light to see that far.

Halfway up the hillside, Naste began to whine and carry on. He looked at Piera. Piera pushed off with his pole and started downhill. He went down the steep decline so fast that he almost lost control, skied all the way to the bottom. From here there was a gorge with a stream that lead to Áiteskaidi. On both sides, frost-covered mountain walls rose into the air. It was all like a Stallo castle. The crunching of the snow under Naste's feet echoed between the cliffs. The light in the chasm was dim. The stream seemed almost dry. Some distance ahead rose a wall of rock, an overhanging cliff under which no snow had gathered. The cliff stood there, dark, like a door into the mountain.

Naste stopped. The hair on his back bristled. He began to bark violently, the sound ringing through the mountains. He barked at the hollow wall that looked like a door. More and more ferociously he bayed at this door as he moved closer and finally disappeared behind a rock just by the opening.

Piera seized his rifle and aimed. Naste whined and barked, his barking breaking into long howls. All Piera could see was snow being kicked up behind the rock, and he heard the snapping of teeth. Naste howled, howled so that the sound rang through the mountains, and then he leaped out from behind the rock and came back to Piera. Piera could see one shadow and then another move quickly along the mountain wall.

97

His rifle thundered. Just one shot. He heard howling and whi-ning. Snow flew around in all directions at the dark door opening.

Piera looked around, listened, and squinted to see better. The mountain walls boomed, and the wolves lay in the cold snow, grow-ling their litany of death. Naste barked and whimpered. At times, he barked intensely, only to stop again. Piera looked at the dog. It held one of its front feet up above the snow. It was injured. Piera hopped out of his skis, grabbed Naste and examined him. Naste whined and quivered.

"Vuoi, poor dog… that you've hurt your foot. The bone must be broken, and you're bleeding, too." He put Naste down on his coat. His rifle in his hand, he waded through the deep snow to the base of the cliff. Two big bodies were stretched out beside each other on top of red snow, their tongues hanging out. Piera skinned them while they were still warm. Naste tried to come over, but he constantly got stuck when his healthy foot broke through the crusted snow. Piera tossed the wolf skins over his shoulder and trudged back to Naste.

Then he set off on his skis. Naste hobbled behind, whining and wagging his tail at the same time. But he moved ever so slowly. In that way they finally reached the house. The moon had disappeared behind Njiejatanvárri. The valley was cast in shadow, but the moun-tain tops still shone with a faint red glow in the pale moonlight

Piera let Naste into the house. Alone, he went to look for the reindeer. He followed their tracks. They had scrambled up the hill, and up there he could hear the clattering of a bell.

Dawn came at last. Smoke rose through the cold mist.

The snow stars slowly faded. The Arctic winter twilight spread its red glow across the horizon. It was in this light that Máhtte moved along Geavu with his herd of reindeer. Their journey, with its yelling and grunting, clanging and clamoring, could be heard from far away. At the very back, the train of draft reindeer and sleds came crackling on. Dogs were barking. Now and then a child's cry could be heard.

Biehtar and the bell reindeer were in the lead. Piera stayed with the sleds. Máhtte himself was standing on his sled behind the herd, yoiking and yelling to the reindeer to move on. But his voice barely reached Biehtar through the even, rushing sound of the herd. Only half of him was visible above the steam from the breath of the running reindeer.

Thus they moved through the narrow river valley. Past headlands and islets. The sounds they made traveled far and told people that now they were on their way.

There were buildings on the riverbanks, on the open fields, and at the edge of the birch woods. Here the Sami had settled and struggled for food in a landscape that the frost had tormented. In the middle of the brushwood or in a clearing beside the bog, at the edge of a swamp, on a field of heather or a moss-covered ridge, nature had yielded places for them. And from this the meadows had grown forth.

Máhtte was thinking about all this as he moved past the buildings. Surrounded by tumult, Máhtte traveled along Geavu toward the winterland.

From Koccam spalli, *1940*
Translated by Roland Thorstensson

Oktyabrina Voronova

Our Life

Oktyabrina Voronova (1934–1990) was born in a small settlement with the poetic name "Eyes turned toward the forest" in the far eastern part of the Kola Peninsula. This community was abandoned in the 1960s, because the Russian authorities felt that it offered no possibilities for development. Voronova studied at the Herzen Pedagogical Institute in St. Petersburg and worked as a librarian in Revda. She published three collections of poetry in Russian, always wishing, however, to use her native language to give expression to her experience of a life close to nature with the reindeer herders on the tundra. She wrote in the Ter dialect, one of the easternmost of all the Sami dialects. She continued to work on *Yealla* [Life], a collection of poetry, right up until her death in 1990. This book was published posthumously and is now in the process of being translated to Northern Sami, the dialect which the majority of Sami people read and write.

Words

$\mathcal{E}$ACH WORLDLY THING SOUNDS DIFFERENTLY,
all objects have their names.
So these too have their designations:
sun, tundra, hut site,
mother, father, river,
earth and village.
From deep down in the age-old earth
clear waters appeared
a spring opened
and joined word to word.
It's like an old man
who's seen his share of life
remembering his youth…
A silky flame now eats the firewood
and sorrow fills your heart.
You take a stick
and poke the glowing embers.
Up to the point of hurting memories
you call old words to cross your mind:
Sun, Tundra, Water,
Mother, Father, Earth.

The Birch

I N A MEADOW WITH GROWING HAY
there also grows a birch
with its roots that come together
with its top that reaches for the sky.

So they sing their songs,
the people on the move and those not moving.
The Komi and the Sami come together
to celebrate a holy day.

They approach the birch
and embellish it with gifts,
who gives a bead,
who gives some other pretty thing.

They dance around the birch tree singing
like the water in a brook.
The tundra people chant their chants
in a language shared by everyone.

For those who don't submit to worries,
through the ages and in times to come,
like the roots of the birch tree
the earth provides for each and every one.

The Echo

*T*HE MOUNTAIN FOREST BECAME EMPTY,
You shiver in the autumn chill.
How long will the cold still last?
And the echo answers:
– Years… years…

The trees dream of their green clothing,
You look for berries, mushrooms, but in vain.
You think there should be some.
And the echo answers:
– There were… there were…

Long ago the cuckoo told your years to you,
Your summers that were hidden in the clouds.
Sun and warmth – where did they go?
And your empty head just groans.
And the echo answers:
– Somewhere… somewhere…

Be still, you silly imitator.
You should know when to ridicule,
Or why the evenings will be good or bad.
But the echo speaks:
– Storm… Storm…

So what about you, Echo?
I do know
Why rains now will fill the blue sky.
The winter is already on the treshold,
the autumn will give him no shelter.

Half a hundred

FIFTY. IT'S HALF A HUNDRED.
When I think of it I panic
What is there left for me? –
It was,
     was,
          was…
Oh well…

I kept the fire burning
     in the fire place,
So that there would always be
     a thing or two to eat.
I tended to the cattle,
Gave birth to children.
It was,
     was,
          was…
Oh well.

To grasp a gun, to put the skis on –
I could do it all so easily.
I grew higher on your side, –
It was,

     was,

          was...
Oh well.

No – no place for worries.
Let the past be in the past.
I'm proud to face my age declaring:
Everything that was – is mine!

From Yealla, *1990*
Translated by Pekka Sammallahti

Paulus Utsi

As Long As We Have Waters

Paulus Utsi (1918–1975) became a writer one step at a time. He was primarily a reindeer herder and craftsman. Utsi taught Sami *duodji* (handicraft) at the Sami Folk High School in Jokkmokk in northern Sweden for a number of years. This school was one of the hotbeds of revitalization of Sami crafts and culture, which began around 1970. As adviser of many enthusiastic young people who sought admission to the school in Jokkmokk, Utsi played a central role in this process, and, in a way, he had the status of "elder" because of his role as a link between tradition and a modern era in Sapmi. Utsi could address the Sami's dilemma, based on his own experiences; he had himself been forced to move because of the building of hydroelectric plants, and he had experienced the closing of the border between Norway and Sweden, which prohibited the normal, traditional movement of the reindeer. In his poetry he is occupied with the question of how our modern way of life undermines old values and how the Sami are losing their rights to land and water. But he sees hope in the younger generation and derives strength from a people who preserve their language and traditions. His main source of inspiration, however, is nature in the northern world, where Arctic birch and willow thrive on ground where no plants should be fit to exist.

Nothing

NOTHING STAYS LONGER
in our souls
than the language we inherit
It liberates our thoughts
unfolds our mind
and softens our life

The Shadow

IN THE MOONSHINE I LEAVE
gentle plains behind me
The shadow, the shadow
is my friend
The shadow from the skis
The shadow from the pole
My shadow
follows me
as long as the moon is shining

The Yoik

THE YOIK IS A SANCTUARY FOR OUR THOUGHTS
Therefore it has
few spoken words
Free sounds reach
farther than words

The yoik lifts our spirit
allows our thoughts to soar
above the little clouds
has them
as its friends
in nature's beauty

Reflections
by People of Nature

IN THESE MODERN TIMES
the thoughts of people of nature
are like dust
if something touches them
they turn to nothing
lift
and disappear

They are like the mountain birch
when it is weighed down
and bent
to never again stand erect
IPU

In the Clouds

*I*N THE CLOUDS THE WIND RUNS AMUCK
thinking it can extinguish
the tiny fragile light
But it keeps flickering
giving the Sami
belief in the future and strength
IPU

Little Snail

I SEE A SNAIL
on the mushroom
I bend over
take it in my hand
blow on it
and say
Little snail
let
my reindeer calf
grow horns too
IPU

Shoreless Shore

I DON'T UNDERSTAND ANYTHING
my heart is heavy
Just look around
whole villages are gone
the strangers have fooled us
Their greed has no limit

I stand by a shore
a shoreless shore
Just look around
Old shores are no more
the strangers have robbed them
Their greed has no limit

I see people bend
on an open sea in stormy weather
Just look around
The law is no longer just
the strangers have made their demands
Their greed has no limit

Is see ancestors
who were stubborn and strong
Just look around
We have to suffer great injustices
the strangers violate us
Their greed has no limit
IPU

Yearning

*L*IKE A CROOKED BIRCH TREE
at the edge of the tundra
my life too
is bent by the wind
As the birch longs to reflect light
on patches of bare soil
I long for mountains and plains
summer pastures
This is my life
which I love
IPU

Our Life

*O*UR LIFE
is like a ski track
on the white open plains
The wind erases it
before morning dawns
IPU

As Long
As We Have Waters

*A*s LONG AS WE HAVE WATERS where the fish can swim
As long as we have land where the reindeer can graze
As long as we have woods where wild animals can hide
we are safe on this earth

When our homes are gone and our land destroyed
– then where are we to be?

Our own land, our lives' bread, has shrunk
the mountain lakes have risen
rivers have become dry
the streams sing in sorrowful voices
the land grows dark, the grass is dying
the birds grow silent and leave

The good gifts we have received
no longer move our hearts
Things meant to make life easier
have made life less

Painful is the walk
on rough roads of stone
Silent cry the people of the mountains

While time rushes on
our blood becomes thin
our language no longer resounds
the water no longer speaks

*Poems marked with IPU are co-authored with his wife Inger Huuva Utsi
(1914–1984), who outlived her husband and edited the poems for the second book*
Giela gielain, *1980. The first collection,* Giela giela, *1974, is by PU alone.
Translated by Roland Thorstensson.*

Nils Aslak Valkeapää

The Circle of Life

Nils-Aslak Valkeapää (1943–) does not write about nature, he writes nature; Valkeapää is so much part of life as it truly is lived on the tundra that, in his writing, poetry and nature are one. There is an immediacy in his style of writing; its language and experiential qualities make the reader an active participant in the artistic process. Valkeapää is the first Sami writer to win the prestigious Nordic Prize for Literature, given in recognition of his lyrical photographic work, *Beaivi Áhčážan* [The Sun, My Father]. Valkeapää has completed teacher's training, but he has never taught school, per se. He made his literary debut in 1974 with a collection of poetry, and, in addition to several other collections of poetry, he has also released LP records and CDs with traditional yoik, often combined with jazz and other forms of music. He did this long before world music and ethno-sound became popular. Valkeapää is also an internationally recognized artist, and he has had roles in feature films and TV-series. His poetical work *Ruoktu váimmus*, which he illustrated, has recently been published in English under the title *Trekways of the Wind*.

119

MY HOME IS IN MY HEART
it migrates with me

The yoik is alive in my home
the happiness of children sounds there
herd-bells ring
dogs bark
the lasso hums
In my home
the fluttering edges of gáktis
the leggings of the Sámi girls
warm smiles

My home is in my heart
it migrates with me

You know it brother
you understand sister
but what do I say to strangers
who spread out everywhere
how shall I answer their questions
that come from a different world

How can I explain
that I can not live in just one place
and still live
when I live
among all these tundras
You are standing in my bed
my privy is behind the bushes
the sun is my lamp
the lake my wash bowl

How can I explain
that it moves with me
How can I explain
that others live there too
my brothers and sisters

What shall I say brother
what shall I say sister

They come
and ask where is your home
they come with papers
and say
this belongs to nobody
this is government land
everything belongs to the State
They bring out dingy fat books
and say
this is the law
it applies to you too

What shall I say sister
what shall I say brother

You know brother
you understand sister

But when they ask where is your home
do you answer them all this
On Skuolfedievvá we pitched our lavvo
during the spring migration
Čáppavuopmi is where we built our goahti during rut
Our summer camp is at Ittunjárga
and during the winter our reindeer are in Dálvadas

You know it sister
you understand brother

Our ancestors kept fires on Allaorda
on Stuorajeaggis's tufts
in Viiddesčearru
Grandfather drowned in the fjord while fishing
Grandmother cut her shoe grass in Šelgesrohtu
Father was born in Finjubákti in burning cold

And still they ask
where is your home

They come to me
and show books
Law books
that they have written themselves
This is the law and it applies to you too
See here

But I do not see brother
I do not see sister
I cannot
I say nothing
I only show them the tundra

I see our fjelds
the places we live
and hear my heart beat
all this is my home
and I carry it
within me
in my heart

I can hear it
when I close my eyes
I can hear it

I hear somewhere
deep within me
I hear the ground thunder
from thousands of hooves
I hear the reindeer herd running
or is it the noaidi drum
and the sacrificial stone
I discover
somewhere within me
I hear sound whisper shout call
with the thunder still echoing
from rib to rib

And I can hear it
even when I open my eyes
I hear it

Somewhere deep within me
I can hear it
a voice calling
and the blood's yoik I hear
In the depths
from the dawn of life
to the dusk of life

All of this is my home
these fjords rivers lakes
the cold the sunlight the storms
The night and day of the fjelds
happiness and sorrow
sisters and brothers
All of this is my home
and I carry it in my heart

From Ruoktu vaimmus, *1985,* Trekways of the Wind, *1994*
Translated by Ralph Salisbury, Lars Nordström, and Harald Gaski

Kirsti Paltto

Looking Back

Kirsti Paltto (1947–) has behind her a long and multifaceted literary career as a writer of novels, short stories, poetry, children's books, and radio plays. A number of Paltto's short stories are particularly interesting from a purely stylistic point of view as examples of literature in transition from an oral to a written culture. Her first published work, *Soagŋu* [The Proposal Journey], from 1971, includes short stories that are actually told in the same manner as they have been told orally by many generations. Moreover, *Soagŋu* is the first book written in the Sami language by a woman. Kirsti Paltto has been an active participant in organizational work for Sami artists and was the first chairperson of the Sami Writers' Association, founded in 1979. She lives in the vicinity of Ohcejohka, one of the northernmost communities in Finland, which lies on Europe's best salmon stream, the Tana River.

*T*ODAY IS THE OFFICIAL DAY OF MOURNING. It's Sunday, and the sunlight is so strong that the snow glitters. But I can't arouse any mourning in my heart, it will not even stir. When I woke up early this morning, I was calm and felt that nothing tied me down any more. It was as though a long captivity were over, as if I finally were a free human being who had the right to think my own thoughts.

It's true that my conscience needles me and begs me to mourn, but even though I prayed to God last night that I would feel grief, I never have. And I never will.

I was only a young girl of sixteen when I came to the farm as a servant. I sat, shy and lonely, on the chopping block by the door just after Father had cracked the whip and driven off, leaving me all alone at this strange farm. The farmer's wife poured coffee for me and asked me to come to the table. I walked up to it, looking at no one. The farmer spoke to me. I answered quietly, my eyes fixed on the table. That's how shy I was.

But although I was shy, I had a good disposition, and both talking and laughing came easily to me as soon as I got to know people. The people on the farm were religious, and the farmer himself would travel around to preach at meetings. All their kinsmen were known for their Christian and God-fearing ways. And some of them lived here at Njáigoguolban, where I came this winter day forty-two years ago. They needed a girl who was willing to work, and I fit that description.

Without grumbling, I did everything they told me. Without ever complaining, I was both milk-maid and nurse-maid on the farm. There was little time for sleeping, and the food rations for the servant girl were short. Miserly they were, like all the rest of the kinsmen, even though the farm was well off. And my wages weren't much either, though I was able to dress up in new shoes after Christmas. But doing that wasn't such a great honor for the children of poor people in those days, it was just a cause for envy.

On the farm lived a handsome bachelor, the family's only son. During the dark winter months, he began to show up in the barn when I was milking, and now and then he shoveled manure out the barn door and gave the cows something to drink. He joked and made me laugh, even though I almost didn't dare – it wasn't proper to laugh in the presence of the heir to the farm. Afterwards I was ashamed of myself. But it was nice, all the same, that someone cared about me. And he cared so much that he began to put his arms around me now and then.

In the winter, when I was done with all the chores the master and mistress of the house had given me, I slept on a sheepskin in the farmhouse. Sometimes I was so tired that I felt faint, and during the night all my limbs ached. Even so, I folded my hands in prayer every evening and thanked God for letting me get work as a servant girl, so that I didn't have to fight for the meager food that was set on the table at home.

That summer I moved out to the storehouse. I carried the bedclothes across the farmyard, where Ásllat made eyes at me as he passed by. I didn't know what he meant, but already the first night he sneaked out into the storehouse and proceeded to lie down next to me. I pushed him out of my bed. He fell against a linen chest and cursed, and then he jumped on top of me. He tore my underpants off and shoved his terribly big stick up into my crotch. He didn't care that I both hit him and cried out, he just laughed. And he didn't care that I moaned in pain when he forced himself into me. He didn't care that I was crying. He finished the job, buttoned his pants, and left.

A week later I began to throw up. I tried to hide it as best I could, but one day, when I was busy washing, the mistress discovered me. In response to her cold questions, I told her the truth.

My goodness, what an uproar it caused! Everybody was convinced that it was my fault that Ásllat had taken me. All the relatives gathered to consider what to do. After one day's deliberation, they had figured out that it was probably best to hide the baby, give it up to someone or other, or send me down to their relatives on the coast so I could give birth to the baby there. They were talking as if I didn't even exist. And, finally, they agreed that I should go to the coast, where I wouldn't bring shame on their family because of my bastard. Miserable, I stood up and said that I would rather go home than to strangers on the coast.

131

"You just keep your mouth shut," the mistress burst out, adding that I would go down to the coast in the fall, as soon as there was good winter traveling, and until then I had to conceal the circumstance I was in.

"That's how it is," she said emphatically. " We have to protect our own honor. Among our people it's not appropriate that the servant girls have bastards. And don't you even think about running away. We have people who can check up on you, just so you know."

What was I to do? I just sat and felt ashamed of myself.

And thus the summer days went by and fall grew near. I don't know what the family and the rest of the relatives had found out, but one day my master came and ordered me into the side room. There sat Ásllat and my mistress.

"Sire-Elle," my master began, "you work hard and take orders willingly, as if you were made to be a man's wife. You know all there is to know about farm work, and you aren't afraid of exerting yourself, even though you are…. Your presence has been good for the farm, and we have seen that you're a blessing for all of us. You don't ask too much of anyone, but do obediently what's expected of you. Sire-Elle, you were meant to be a wife. Therefore, we'd like to have you marry Ásllat."

"And," my mistress declared, "you should be happy to marry into such a prosperous farm, you who are the daughter of that pauper, Leastto-Jovnna. We take pity on the child you're carrying; it will be our child, born into our family."

I had nothing to say about this; I don't even know if Ásllat had been allowed to express his opinion. But in late September, at about the time of Michaelmas, we began our life together with a big wedding. The bride and groom were like gold and silver, people were saying. All dressed-up and happy.

In February, during the coldest time of winter, I gave birth. A baby girl, a tiny, thin girl, as light as a scrap of fur, came into this world. As for me, conditions weren't any better, now that I had become the daughter in-law on the farm. I worked just as much as before, but now I also had my own baby, who kept me awake at night. I didn't get much sleep, and I became thin and pale. But life had to go on, there was no other way.

Oh, how dearly I loved this little girl, this bit of fur.

I gave her the name Ánnemuorji. I talked and sang and smiled at her when we were alone. Her brown eyes were my suns, and her little hand my support. She was the only one in the house I felt safe around, and she was the only one I talked to. But I always did it in secret, because the others in the house didn't like laughter and chatter. Ásllat often remarked that I spoiled the girl when I made her happy. But, all the same, I couldn't stand to hear Ánnemuorji cry, and I insisted that I be allowed to hold her.

They even forced me to go outside or to another room so that I wouldn't get the child used to being held or sitting on my lap. Children shouldn't do such things; while still in the cradle, they should learn that humans must suffer for their sins. They mustn't get used to life's pleasures early, in their mother's arms. Only when you came to heaven should you expect pleasures and happiness.

Once I was sitting in the upper room, nursing my baby. I sat with my back toward the door, thinking that everyone was outside. I sang for my Ánnemuorji, told her a scary tale about spirits that live underground, and I smiled to her. It was warm and cozy for us, almost heavenly to be alone together. Everything else disappeared and seemed far away. All of a sudden, a person came up behind my back, and before I could react, someone pinched my naked breast, hurting me so much that I almost dropped my baby on the floor.

"Listen, Daughter-in-law, don't raise the child in sin! Don't tell her those old ghost stories, say the Lord's Prayer instead!"

I jumped up, turned around and faced my father-in-law.

Dear God, if only I had dared, I would have given the hypocrite a good one on his ear. I would have whacked him so hard that he would have remembered forever whose breast he had pinched.

But I didn't hit my father-in-law, I just swallowed and felt ashamed of myself. I was close to tears, but I was able to hold them back. I buttoned my sweater and began to make Ánnemuorji's bed ready for her. My father-in-law stood behind me, expounding the words of the Lord, what the Holy Scripture said about wantonness, and what the punishment was for that.

Fortunately, he died that year, that old snake. My mother-in-law wasn't all that bad, at least she didn't pinch my breast, even if she could scold and complain, command and preach about how the wife of her only son really should be.

How happy I was the day we followed mother-in-law's casket to the cemetery. I thought that now Ásllat and I would finally have a real life together.

But oh, no!

Ásllat used his father's and mother's life as an example for us, and he changed and became just like they had been. Day in and day out, he whined about how his mother had been in the habit of doing this or that, what good blood dumplings she used to make, exactly when she would go to the barn, and so forth. My father-in-law and mother-in-law still lived with us, even though they were dead and buried.

And Ásllat became just as religious as they had been and was busy traveling around, preaching. Often he was away at meetings for weeks, and then I had to take care of the farm and the children. We had a child almost every year, thirteen in all.

When Ásllat was home, he lay in bed or sat at the end of the table and preached and discussed matters with his brothers and sisters in faith. I cooked and made coffee and set everything on the table. I was not allowed to be a part of their discussions. A wife was supposed to serve her husband, just as Sarah in the old days had served Abraham. Ásllat never helped me raise the children, he didn't even bother to change the diapers on the little ones when I was in the barn.

Ásllat also forbade me to talk to other women. He had heard that we women badmouthed men and connived, even if, in reality, we just talked about what good husbands we had gotten for ourselves.

I was always tired those years and often cranky with the children. But, gradually, my submissiveness and fear turned to anger. I could hardly stand to see Ásllat's saintly face any longer. Yet I was the mistress of the farm, and half of everything would one day be mine. Therefore, I should have a say, too. And almost as if by chance, that began to happen.

One evening, when I came inside from the barn, Ásllat was sitting by the stove together with Vielte-Jovnása Máret, a woman from a place nearby. He sat there, red in his face, interpreting the Scriptures. The two of them were so absorbed in the words of the Lord that they didn't notice at all when I came in, even though I rattled the milk buckets and made a racket throwing them down on the table. It began to seethe within me, like in an all too full pot of porridge that is ready to boil – yes, not just boil, but boil over. Then I caught sight of the water dipper that was lying there so conveniently. I reached down with it into the bucket and filled it with ice-cold water, which I threw right into Ásllat's and Máret's faces.

There was one heck of a row! Ásllat shot up like an arrow, even though he was in the middle of the Scriptures, and he could have

135

attacked me, but he didn't really dare to begin fighting with me in front of Máret. Still, he called me crazy and snorted and sputtered before finally going outside, leaving Máret, his spiritual friend, behind.

I laughed a devilish, scornful laugh.

Afterwards Ásllat slapped me. During the night, when the children were asleep. He certainly could have beaten me black and blue, but I scratched and bit him in the face. Many years went by like that. I became more and more hardened and quarrelsome. I became indifferent. I couldn't stand my husband any longer. We fought, and I could have killed both him and myself. But I didn't kill anyone, and for that reason, too, I became so full of hate. Completely. I, who had been so soft and tender when I was young, now gritted my teeth and hated. And I worked as hard as ever before.

Ásllat despised me and had full control over me until he became ill and bed-ridden. He was old, but I was still young and energetic, in my best years.

I suffered, wrangled, and hated for forty-two years. Why? Was that what my life was meant for? What should I have done? Stopped, looked around, and thought of a new course in life? Should I have taken Ásllat by the shoulders, looked him straight in the eye, and asked him why we lived as we did?

I didn't want to submit myself, not even when Ásllat held me during the night and I kept longing for tenderness and a better life, away from the quarrels, away from the hate. I didn't want to, because I was wounded too severely, too deeply.

Deep down, Ásllat was kind, but he had hidden his kindness behind his faith and the Scriptures, and he was too busy trying to follow his parents' teachings and watching out for the sins of others to be able to notice his own. Life could have turned out differently, nevertheless. I could have steeled myself, refused to bicker and use harsh words. I could have been softer. Ásllat was not the only one to blame, but not until now have I been able to admit that.

Now.

Not until now, the official day of mourning. Not until now am I beginning to soften, not until now are my thoughts beginning to work themselves free. I go and get my best clothes out of storage, the clothes in which I was married. I haven't been allowed to wear them, because dressing up was regarded as a sin. I put on the beautiful *gákti*, wrap the silk shawl around my shoulders, fasten it with the brooch, set its fringe in motion. I'm a troll-woman, a woman of the Stories. White fur shoes on my feet, black leggings. A fairy tale woman. A troll-woman. On the border of adventure, the forbidden border of adventure.

Just like the stories we used to tell when I was a child. Here, on this farm, the children grew up without stories. And so our children went out into the world, away from two evil people. They have hardly been back to visit. Four have died. Ánnemuorji is a drunkard in Helsinki. Piera has been in prison four times. Ánde goes around like a good-for-nothing at Oalgenjárga, and Sire is walking the floor in an insane asylum. The others are leading normal lives, whatever that means. Only Katariiná and Máijá have been educated; they are teachers now.

Official day of mourning. But where is my grief? Soon the relatives will come. Soon I'll be ready to follow you on your last journey, Ásllat. You have already been lying in the coffin for a week, but today you'll be buried in consecrated ground.

I am dressed up and prepared to stand at the edge of the grave and watch as they throw sand upon you. I am ready to leave you there and prepared to begin living my own life in the years that I have left on this earth.

From Guovtteoaivvat nisu, *1989*
Translated by Roland Thorstensson

Rauni Magga Lukkari

I Row Across My River

Rauni Magga Lukkari (1943–) is one of the foremost modern Sami poets. She is a native of the Finnish side of the Tana River but has resided in Tromsø in northern Norway for the past 15 years. Lukkari made her debut in 1980. In 1987, she was nominated for the Nordic Council's Prize for Literature for her third published collection of poetry, *Losses beaivegirji* [Dark Journal]. In 1991 she published a bilingual collection of poetry in Sami and Norwegian, *Mu gonagasa gollebiktasat/Min konges gylne klær* [My King's Golden Clothes]. Her most recent work to date is another bilingual poetry book in Sami and Finnish, *Čalbmemihttu* [Visual estimate], 1995. Lukkari has also written for the Sami theater, Beaivváš, based in Guovdageaidnu/Kautokeino, Norway, and has been a sought-after writer of introductions for important Sami occasions, such as the opening sessions of the Sami Parliament in Karasjok and the Sami College in Kautokeino in 1989.

I ROW ACROSS MY RIVER
Father's river
Grandfather's river
Row first to the Norwegian side
then to the Finnish side
I row across my river
to Mother's side
Father's side
Wondering
where homeless children belong

*

Tomorrow she will leave for school
for a strange life
with a child's fragile happiness
Anxiety tears at my throat
the memories
of my own first day at school
sting

*

I stroke her silken hair
am filled with sorrow
how will she manage
in this foreign world
How can I guide her
when I myself have gone astray

*

141

I envy people
who can adorn life
and live like ducks
on the surface of the water

*

I awaken to foreign words
see shameless lies
in unfamiliar eyes
feel heavy hands
against my skin
Still, I creep closer
to disappear deeper

*

But when it is not *he*
with his hands
without lies in his eyes
not he
with words that I know

*

For
if you leave now
I will not find you again.
For
if you really yield
I will walk past.
And lose my way

*

He has gone
to strangers
he is dead
among the strange ones
He departed
in dawn's early light
at the break of day
before the birds
awakened
I am alone
restless
with my love

*

I had prayed
for the pine forest's heavy silence
wished for the swan's gliding wings
the fish's eyes
and instead of this restless heart
I wanted a smooth stone

*

I have gone so far away
that I almost find my way
The alien familiar
my brother closer
my mother's hand warmer
washed in strange words
Paths open up
with the flood
toward the unknown sea

143

Linked together
by love, we two.
I do not escape you
On our point
the river's roar is not muted.
It rushes like your blood.
The grass damp
beneath your feet.
You remember the summers, don't you.
How high the clouds drifted.
The storehouse roof
sky-high above its beam.

                    *

I am no more
than halfway.
For the first time now
I am ready to depart.
To begin
my own
journey

                    *

You
stand in the middle
of my life
like a pillar.
If I fell you
I will be
without feet

                    *

144

If one doesn't sleep during the sunlit nights
the long winter will provide time enough

*

I knew
you wouldn't return.
Since the sun shone
right after
you left

*

Nights and days
I hold back the rain.
I let the clouds fall
between the birches.

*

My king's clothes
shine like gold.
Stars from the sky
on his belt
beneath his chin
adorning his back.
What else can I do
but walk softly behind
rest my eyes
on my hands'
accomplishment

From Jieŋat vulget, *1980,* Báze dearvan, Biehtár, *1981,* Losses beaivegirji, *1986*
and Mu gonagasa gollebiktasat/Min konges gylne klær, *1991.*
Translated by Edi Thorstensson

Synnøve Persen

Along
a Windless Path

Synnøve Persen (1950–) was born and raised in Porsanger, one of the five fjord districts in Finnmark. Persen received her training at the National Art Academy in Oslo and was first recognized primarily as a visual artist. In recent years, she has firmly established herself as a poet. Her collection of poetry from 1992, *biekkakeahtes bálggis* [windless path], was the Sami entry for the Nordic Council's Prize for Literature in 1993. Persen has also played a very central part in organizational work promoting Sami art and culture, arguing strongly for the establishment of a separate Nordic Sami art museum in Kárášjohka/Karasjok, Norway, where the Norwegian Sami parliament, Sámediggi, convenes.

SILENT ROOMS

fall
leaves

*

are falling
along a windless
path

*

did a star
pass by
did anything
happen

*

if the sun
were shining
on the other side
of the moon

*

bend
the bow
so that it
reaches

*

between the heavens
homeless
in the maelstrom

*

on the water's edge
I find
the bluish-red shell

*

while the wind
booms
and the waves break

*

golden sun
comes
and
goes

*

I am swimming
in
the morning sky
greeting
the clouds

*

150

the ocean
is reaching
for your beams

*

the night birds are calling
do I
dare

*

the secret of the ocean
moonbeam
kissing you

*

mountains are thawing
silk oceans are bursting

*

the tender beginning
of dreams
the ski-tracks
on snowy slopes

*

151

black trees
are scratching
the wounds

the mountains are asleep

*

the moon
the sun
the stars
are
the floating river

*

the ocean is moving
the sky is whispering

*

opening the sky
I bang on the door

*

152

stroke the threads
time
glides

*

the mountains
are open
singing without sound

*

the ocean wind
is mustering the memories

for prayer

*

bright night
soft wind

among the birches you whistle

*

little rivers rustle in my heart
ice melting
turning into joy

*

153

your beautiful best coat
silver in your belt

silver in your hair
stars in your eyes

you shine
holding my hand

       *

I hear your voice
the words golden smoke
rising in the sky

       *

night sun golden mountain
the birches are calling
come!
young green leaves
are sweet

       *

streaks of gold above the mountain
my dear
the day is being born
and between us
is skin

       *

blue is the night
stars are sparkling

you ask me where I was

a guest with the stars
for five nights

*

words cannot tell
if I love

these mountain plains
entrance me

From biekkakeahtes bálggis, *1992 and* alit lottit girdilit, *1981*
Translated by Gerd Bjørhovde

Eino Guttorm

On Bloodied Paths

Eino Guttorm (1941–) is one of several writers from Tana Valley. He comes from the Finnish side of the valley, where for some distance the Tana river constitutes the border between Finland and Norway. Guttorm is primarily a novelist and a writer of short stories, but he has also written some comedies for a regional theater group. In addition to being a writer, Guttorm is a carpenter and craftsman. Like many of his fellow authors, Guttorm grew up in a culture where the tradition of story-telling was held in high esteem. Influences from this tradition are particularly noticeable in Guttorm's short stories, which are full of potent language and exuberance. The oral tradition is most evident in Guttorm's dialog, in which the writer's use of hyperbole, understatement, and luxuriant metaphors create images that almost come to life.

*W*INTER WAS OVER and spring arrived. One frosty night, Gáisá and Aleks set off to hunt wild reindeer. They climbed the steepest side of Bealljevárri and came up on the bare mountain. Aleks took Gáisá by the hand and let his glance glide over the wide expanses below, which were barely distinguishable from the sky in the early morning light, and further down to the bottom of the valley, where the earth hut lay curled up in a ball between tall birch trees. It looked like a hare's turd in the the middle of the endless landscape.

"Can't we be man and wife?" Aleks asked and put his arm around Gáisá's shoulder.

Gáisá jumped, tore herself free, and moved to the side.

159

"Now, what's this?" Aleks exclaimed and grasped her hand again. "I may ask that question, may I not…, when I'm more fond of you than I've ever been of anyone."

"I can't. What would happen to Mother? And, besides, I'm afraid there would be the same worries if I become tied to a man."

"You wouldn't be tied down because of that, and your mother is so old, she might drop any day…. Then you'll be all alone on Bealljevárri if I leave."

I'm not afraid of being alone. I'm used to that. If I want company, I just whistle in the woods. There I have all the company I need."

"But you do need a man."

"I don't know. I think I've already shed enough tears because of men," Gáisá replies cautiously, and she pulls her hand back again.

"Do you really want me to leave? Now when we could have had it so good. Right now, when we could have settled down and created that which is part of life: a home, children….

"Children?" Gáisá cried and started running. Aleks ran after, grabbed hold of her arm and pulled her down. She couldn't get away, however much she kicked.

"I didn't mean to scare you, stupid girl. I won't talk about it anymore, either. You just stay here until you get tired of it and start hunting for me. I'm a pretty decent guy after all, aren't I?"

"Let me go… let me go," Gáisá groaned. "We have to move on before the snow's crust begins to melt. The sun will soon rise, it's already morning."

Then they took off.

* * *

No more words were exchanged about the matter. Aleks couldn't stop wondering about this Gáisá. What kind of person was she who wouldn't yield and didn't show the least sign of happiness, even when he talked to her so nicely? Such sweet talk would have made any other maiden jump for joy.

God, what a strange old woman… she already has one foot in the grave, doesn't understand a word of what's said to her, and yet the old witch knows that no man can get into bed with Gáisá, he thought, and he looked out of the corner of his eye at Bikká who sat on the edge of the bed, laughing to herself, her eyes moving back and forth like those of an idiot. Every time Aleks manages to catch her eye, she giggles and behaves like a little girl, pursing her lips and stroking her hair.

I think I'm going to have to strangle that troll before fall comes, Aleks thought, I'm sure I'll find a way to do away with her. Exactly how he didn't know, however.

"Why do you sit there and brood so much? What are you thinking about?" Gáisá asked. Aleks scowled at Bikká but collected himself and stuttered that he was thinking about the people at home.

"I wonder if they still remember me."

"What do you think they would've said if they'd known you were a foster child here?" Gáisá remarked, straightening her back and throwing out her chest, as if to show that she was enough of a woman to call Aleks a child.

Aleks weighed the words. Foster child. He remained sitting a while, looking away, before he answered.

"You're the only one who regards me as a child. You're free to call me that in your arrogance, but you'll see. I'm sure you'll call me a man some day… and husband."

"I'll have a say in that matter, too."

"What if I showed you that I am a man?"

161

"How would you do that?"

"Really show you. Seriously…, you troll from hell."

"What good would that do? Playing husband…."

"You'll see!" Aleks screamed and stormed out of the house.

"No devil will get to touch me," Gáisá yelled after him.

"Aaa, ah, a," gasped Bikká as though she was about to choke, and she came over to her daughter in one leap and pointed to the door.

"Latch the door, so he won't come in, hee, hee. Just lock it, and he'll probably go his way."

"I'm not going to latch the door! I'll show him that I'm a grown person who does what she wants to do."

Aleks didn't come inside until late in the evening. He found his bed, crawled under the covers, and fell asleep without saying a word.

The next morning he was as cheerful as ever. As if nothing had happened.

That was the first time Gáisá understood that he was harboring evil plans, because he seemed to take everything in stride. She surmised from his patience that he was probably going to try other courses of action. She could expect anything.

Aleks was waiting for an opportunity to get Bikká out of the way. It was all perfectly clear to him, and he had no bad conscience about it whatsoever. Only one thing occupied his mind: that Gáisá would have to give in as soon as Bikká was dead.

* * *

Finally the moment he had been waiting for arrived. Gáisá told him she was planning a trip down to the river, and she didn't expect to be back until evening. She asked Aleks if he wanted to come along, but he answered that he didn't have the least interest in seeing either

Biera Heandarat or any of the others he had stayed with last fall. But when Gáisá asked him why, he couldn't come up with a real answer, he just stuttered.

Aleks sat outside the hut and watched Gáisá leave. He became completely breathless when he thought about soon being able to fondle her round buttocks and breasts. But his heart also beat with fear at the thought of Bikká's writhing body and the sounds of her death throes.

Gáisá will soon be down at the riverbank, he said to himself as he prepared to carry out his plan. His hands were sweaty, and beads of perspiration formed on his brow. His mouth and cheeks quivered as he sneaked into the hut. Bikká was sitting there, completely unaware, tapping her cane against the floor. She laughed her idiot's laugh when he came in, her final laugh. She still didn't sense any danger and showed no fear when Aleks came toward her. Didn't grow suspicious when he stopped in front of her bed, either. She had barely enough time to react when Aleks pulled her off the bed, grabbed her by her legs, and twisted her head against her left shoulder. It seemed so easy. But a thin neck can be tough, and even though he twisted it almost all the way around, he was unable to break it. Bikká flung her arms around and howled, her eyes rolled so that only their whites were visible. As tough as an old cat, Aleks thought, and twisted her neck even more. He couldn't let go, he knew that. Her neck was now so damaged that there was barely any life left in the old woman. It wasn't that easy to kill a person. Aleks realized that now. His arms were exhausted, the sounds went through marrow and bone, and his conscience made his hands tremble as time went on.

"Hell," he swore behind clenched teeth, pulled her closer and pressed her head under his arm full force. The sounds she made cut through him like knives. Her glances did the same. Finally, her arms dropped.

163

Carefully, Aleks let the body fall to the floor. He was prepared to run away, but also ready to attack again, if there was still a hint of life in her. He straightened himself up, drenched in sweat. He was unable to think any longer, he didn't know what to do. Felt like he had to get outside, but the door seemed so far away, almost unreachable. It was quiet in the hut. Yet Aleks stood there with his hands over his ears to keep the noise out. His heart was pumping so much blood to his head that there were buzzing and rushing sounds in his ears. It was as though the hut was full of all kinds of sounds. From the depths of his conscience, wherever that may dwell, someone called, and the voice was Bikká's.

"Killer, murderer!" the voice yelled without stopping.

Finally, Aleks came to his senses enough to get out of the hut. Outside, the sun was shining, the sparrows were twittering in all kinds of languages. Aleks paid no attention. How to escape was the only thing on his mind. Run, flee, anywhere. South toward his home, north to the sea, into the forest, far into the dense brush. But he never got going. Just remained standing there, looking around to see if the devil would soon appear and gobble him up.

Aleks repeated to himself that it was much better for Bikká to die than to live. Still, his hands kept trembling, and her screams continued to resound in his ears. What was Gáisá going to say? Would she believe that her mother's heart had stopped? Would she examine her throat, see that her head was too limp?

In a daze, he began walking toward where Gáisá had gone, to meet her. It would be best if she knew before she came home. Then her suspicions wouldn't be aroused as easily. He followed the path she had taken. The whole time he was hoping that she would appear. At the same time he was hoping she would never come home. Then he would get out of having to explain, then he would be spared the fear of being discovered.

When he saw the river, he stopped. From here he could see the path all the way to the door of Biera Heanderat's hut. Here he would spot her as soon as she came out and started her trip home.

He waited and waited. But he only saw little children running between Ánte's and Biera's huts.

Finally, some grownups came out. He saw that Gáisá was one of them. She didn't seem to be in a hurry. Aleks became angry and let loose a long oath, relegating Biera Heanderat to the hottest part of hell for detaining the girl so long. His pangs of conscience turned into hate, and he wished death on everyone along the entire river.

"I should have skewered them all on the same knife, the whole pack of lazy bums from hell. If there had been nicer people around here, everything would have been different. Why the hell should I get myself tangled up in this…, why should I seek the company of idiots?"

Aleks raved and swore at both himself and the others. He didn't quite know why, but he went on swearing until Gáisá had come close to him.

"You finally had sense enough to leave," he mumbled when she came up to where he was standing.

"Finally? Why? Anyway, what business is it of yours where I am and how long I stay? Who has asked you to look after me and follow me around?" Gáisá replied in just as cold a voice.

"I'm not just following you around, I came because I was getting bored staying with a dead person."

"Who are you calling a dead person?"

"Someone who's dead. I left because your mother stopped breathing, and she's not stirring, either. She just lies completely still, next to the bed."

At first Gáisá didn't quite understand what he had said, it seemed so incredible; therefore she blurted out without thinking:

"You miserable Finn, you've killed her, haven't you?" That was more than Aleks could take. His blood was boiling, and he reached for his knife.

"I haven't killed anyone yet, but I'll soon do it, if you don't take back what you said."

"I didn't mean it. I was thoughtless, but right away you pull your knife."

"Yes. When you ask for it… when you accuse me… of course I do."

Gáisá didn't have the strength to argue any longer. She sensed that Aleks had told her the truth, and she began to hurry. She half ran all the way home, so she could see for herself.

"Did you tell me the truth?" she asked cautiously, before they went inside. Her sorrowful glance made Aleks tremble again, and in a hoarse voice he answered, "Yes."

Aleks expected Gáisá to run into his arms for comfort when she saw her lifeless mother, and then, he thought, he would be allowed to caress her where she was the softest. But she didn't jump into his arms. Without saying a word, she looked at the body lying there, strangely contorted and half propped against the bed. A few times she stroked her mother's hair, and then she placed the body on its side. Then she backed up toward the door and disappeared.

When Aleks had come out into the yard, she had already run a good distance and didn't answer his calls.

"Hell. Hell and damnation!" he yelled after her, but Gáisá didn't turn around. She ran and ran until he couldn't see her any longer.

From Varahuvvan bálgát, *1985*
Translated by Roland Thorstensson

Jovnna-Ánde Vest

The Cloudberry Trip

Jovnna-Ánde Vest (1948–) was born in a small Sami community in the Tana River valley. For many years, however, he, his French wife, and their son have made their home in Paris, where he earns his living as an author and translator, as well as an editor for the Sami language periodical *Sápmelaš*, which is published in Finland. Vest attended the University of Helsinki in Finland. He won the first Sami fiction competition, held in 1988, with a biographical novel about his father, who died in a plane crash on his way to a Sami conference during the 1970s. By describing episodes from childhood, the author draws a portrait of his father as an outsider in his own world, yet somehow a representative of that world. The depiction becomes as well a picture of a small, rural Sami community at the time when great social, economic, and cultural changes were rapidly taking place in the north. This is a time when the automobile, motorcycle, and phonograph make their appearance in Sapmi.

*I*N SAPMI, picking cloudberries has always been considered men's work, while gathering other berries has been left to the women and children. Lingonberry and blueberry patches were located close enough to the houses that even the youngest children could get to them, but the cloudberry bogs were usually pretty far off the beaten track. The women didn't have the time and the youngsters didn't have the endurance to walk that far. It was the same in our family. As long as we kids were too little to come along, Father did the cloudberry picking alone. Mother had more than enough other work to do. Father was a persistent cloudberry gatherer, but I can't remember a single time when he so much as covered the bottom of a pail with either lingonberries or blueberries.

For Father, cloudberry picking was not simply a matter of filling pails and tubs with berries. It was much more. It was the suspence of snooping around in the marshes during the summer and seeing whether it promised to be a good year; and nothing could compare with the peace he found in nature. We knew of many bogs where there were plenty of cloudberries, if it was any kind of year for them. But Father wasn't the least bit interested in those bogs. He wanted to search out his own. A lot of berries went unpicked because he had to do things his own way. Time was spent wandering around, looking.

"You should go to Biesjeaggi, too; there are enough berries there," suggested Mother.

"Everybody else is picking loads of berries along the road, but Jovnna, he tries to run away from the cloudberries," Grandmother remarked.

Father wasn't one of those who let themselves be persuaded; he went exactly where he himself intended.

It was a good year for cloudberries, and people were picking great quantities of berries right by the road. Father decided to head for Gápmasjohka. According to what he had heard, the real cloudberry bogs were there.

Once before, we had drifted in our famous aluminum boat all the way down Giellájohka to Gápmasjohka and a good ways further. We were out after cloudberries that time, too. When the supplies began to run low, we had to struggle our way back with our gear. I remember how stiff my muscles were when we finally reached the road after three days and nights of rowing. By then we had figured out that our aluminum boat wasn't really so well suited to the rapids.

We had grown much wiser since that trip. This time we tied the flat-bottomed river boat onto the truck and, in addition, we brought along the Mercury outboard. So that we could go down the parts of the river where the current was slow, Father said. We had outfitted ourselves properly: enough food supplies, plus fishing poles as well as nets. This time we planned on going far enough down Gápmasjohka that we would meet up with the road again.

This cloudberry trip has secured itself extra well in my memory. It happened several years after our house had burned down. Father was always irritable when he was home. We had to weigh our words carefully around him. The relationship between the two of us was already pretty bad. I could hardly stand to talk with him. But I had noticed that he became calmer when he got away from home.

We were out, trying our luck, on the very first day. There were berries all over, even if you couldn't exactly say that they were in abundance. When it began to grow dark, we dragged ourselves back to the boat. We got ready for the night and lit a campfire. Our stomachs were growling with hunger; we hadn't had time to eat a decent meal all day.

How well I remember that mild evening. Father had looked for a stick on which to hang the kettle over the fire, and soon the coffee was on. Then he started roasting salmon. We had brought along both fresh river salmon and smoked salmon. Father whittled roasting sticks for the youngest children and showed us how to fasten the salmon on the stick so that it would stay put. After that, he showed us which side to roast first, in order that the fish wouldn't slide off. "So you kids will know how, for when you are on your own out in the marsh," he said, mostly to himself. Patiently he taught us little tricks that are indispensible in the wilderness. The next day, he showed us how easy it is to get dwarf birch to burn. He stopped right in the middle of the marsh and boiled coffee, just to demonstrate this for us.

"Don't you kids go and think that the only thing mountain people have to work with are juniper and dry willow."

Now he was a father who was preparing his children for life. It was amazing to see how a person who was so grumpy and short-tempered at home was capable of all this.

Darkness fell. We could hear the rushing sound of a little waterfall further downstream. It was so safe and good to sit here with Father as he quietly, peacefully told stories about different things that had happened in his life.

A strange screech out in the marsh awakens me. The others have heard it, too.

"Pappa! What was that?" asks Piera-Niilas, frightened.

"It's the cranes making a racket now in the fall," is all Father says, and he turns onto his other side.

Once we know this, we quiet down and fall asleep again. It was on that trip that I saw both cranes and whooper swans for the first time.

Father was good-natured and patient the whole time. We soon realized that we had brought along far too many empty buckets. We would never manage to fill them all. Father didn't mind so much that there weren't many berries in some of the bogs. Even that had its good side: nobody else came there. He didn't like it when strangers came around. If they did, he would clear out fast. If he so much as saw people's footprints, it was the same. He would hurry to get away. It made no difference if there were plenty of berries to be had.

We kept on searching and picking along the river for a week. It was a dry fall, and the boat barely floated down the shallow stretches. The motor was nothing but a nuisance, since we had to haul the boat along the river bank past the worst spots. Father's long, gently-flowing stretches of river had shrunk noticeably. We no doubt could have picked many times the cloudberries in the same amount of time, had we picked along the road back home, but as a learning experience, our trip was more than successful. I have often since heard my brothers and sisters refer to "that time we went with Father to Gápmasjohka."

Perhaps a person wouldn't think that trips to pick cloudberries are especially meaningful incidents in people's lives, but, for us, they became just that. So, if I want to provide a description of our existence, I can't leave them out.

I learned a great deal on these trips. For one thing, I got to know Father better. At home he was generally disagreeable and spoke very little. But as soon as he got to the marsh, he was like a new person. His problems let go their hold on him, and, for a short time, he could enjoy life.

I noticed what a good storyteller he was. There were neither stallos nor ghosts in his stories, and he didn't tell war stories where someone kills ten Russians with one bullet. He told about ordinary people's little experiences, but he described them so vividly that a person became completely absorbed.

One morning, as we sat drinking coffee before we headed out into the marsh, he began to tell about a fellow (possibly Inggá-Piera, I no longer remember) who came across wolverine tracks and set off in pursuit on his skis. The wolverine was moving right along in the loose snow, but so was the man. When the wolverine discovered that something was after him, it sped up even more. Figured it would be easy to outdistance the man in those snow conditions. That had worked before, and it scarcely occured to the wolverine that it might be in greater danger this time. But that's where it was fooled. It didn't know that the predator chasing it this time was someone who had hunted wolverines before and knew that they, too, are mortal creatures.

173

"Oh well," all of a sudden Father cut himself off, "shall we get going?"

"Aren't you going to finish the story?" we begged.

"There's so much, I can't finish it all at one time. But when we stop for lunch, I'll try to tell the rest."

So that's as far as we got with the wolverine hunt for the time being. We trudged out into the bog, our day packs on our backs. Later, when we sat down again to eat lunch, we waited, full of suspense, for the story to continue.

"You have to tell us more," the youngest ones fret, so eager that they all cry out at the same time.

"Let's see now, what was I telling about?" asks Father, and he doesn't let on that he remembers.

"About the wolverine and the man!"

"Oh, that's right. The wolverine and the man. How far had we gotten?"

We tell him that the wolverine knows now that the man is after it, and it is fleeing at a tremendous pace.

"That's what it was… sure, that's what it was," smiles Father, and then he begins.

The wolverine moves on through the forest, stopping now and then to listen. Stands there and looks back in the direction of its tracks. All around, it is completely still. Then, ominous creaking and cracking sounds can be heard. The man is getting closer. The wolverine has to move on. It feels a new and strange uneasiness. This man is different from the others; he is aided by evil powers. The wolverine takes shorter and shorter rests. But it still isn't tired.

New landscape: valleys, crevasses, mountain peaks. Expanses that offer a good view of the distance. The wolverine knows this terraine and chooses its course. Now it is going to leave the man behind for good. But, at the other end of the plateau, the man in the

174

gákti appears again. His fur coat is tied on his shoulders. Now the wolverine can see its enemy for the first time. A shiver runs down its spine. Its arrogance fades. It knows that it is fighting for its life, and the only avenue of escape lies straight ahead. But it isn't as easy to run in the fresh snow now as it was in the beginning.

Father stops there and calmly rolls himself a cigarette. Lights it, takes a long drag. We wait for the story to continue. But he looks as though he has forgotten everything around him; sits there, lost in thought. We have to arouse him, bring him back. Then he starts up again. At first he doesn't remember where he left off, and it takes him a while to pick up those fresh wolverine tracks again. As we head back to the marsh, the man has just spotted the wolverine, but then it quickly turns up a scree and disappears into the mountains.

By the time we sit down by the tent in the evening, we are dying to hear the end. We quickly ready everything for the night, light the campfire, and prepare our dinner. Then Father goes on with his story.

While we were picking cloudberries, the wolverine has been gathering new strength after its dash up the scree. When at last the man has made it up the mountain, the wolverine immediately slips down into the valley. The man has no choice but to follow. The wolverine is waiting at the bottom, and when the man has finally made his way safely down the precipice, up climbs the wolverine again. They go on like this, over and over.

"Aren't you going to tell us soon whether or not he caught the wolverine?" the youngest of us interrupts the endless tale.

Father doesn't let on that he's heard.

Finally, the wolverine makes a mistake. It leaves the safety of the mountains and heads for open ground. The man follows. The story is picking up speed now. But first we hear more of the same kind of thing we had heard earlier in the day: the wolverine out in

175

front, the man behind. Sometimes the man catches up to within firing range, but by some miracle or other, the wolverine manages to save its hide.

I know that Father is teasing now, trying our patience. So, I just listen and say nothing. The youngest ones don't really catch on to this business of the man's tenacity and the wolverine's incredible luck.

The campfire has almost gone out, when the wolverine switches back behind a mountain peak. Then, suddenly, there is a terrible commotion. The man comes to a dead halt, wonders what in the world it can be. Then he heads toward the sound, moving as fast as he can. And there he sees something strange. An eagle has set its beak into the neck of the wolverine, who is exhausted after two days on the run. The eagle tries to lift the wolverine into the air, but the wolverine has made deep gashes in the eagle's wings with its claws. It has slashed them from base almost to wingtip by the time the man comes gliding up on his skis, his gun over his shoulder. He fires off a couple of shots, and both animals fall to the ground.

"What great luck that guy had," said Toivo one more time as we crept into the tent to gather new strength for the day ahead.

That is the kind of stories Father used to tell on our cloudberry trips. I enjoyed his stories. They were different from the kind I was used to hearing.

Father always had his binoculars along when we were out on one of our trips. Whenever we came to a marsh, he would take a careful look to see if it was worth going in. And if things looked good, we invaded those bogs with our buckets. We went from bog to bog, sometimes without knowing where we were going; or so it seemed, anyway.

176

I remember another time when we sat by the campfire, and Father began to tell a story: He and Ándaras-Ánte and another man were on a cloudberry trip, and they had searched for several days without finding a single thing. They were about to give up and go home, but they agreed to take a quick look at just one more bog before turning back. If there weren't any berries there, either, then they would head straight for home.

They set off. When they reached the edge of the marsh, Ánte took out his binoculars. He peered for quite a while before handing the binoculars over to the next person.

"Look over there, maybe I'm seeing things."

The other fellow lifted the binoculars to his eyes, looked a long time, and said, "It sure is."

"What's out there? Is it cloudberries?" Father cried and grabbed the binoculars.

He searched and found the spot, a fiery red, glowing patch, out in the middle of the bog. Father handed the binoculars back to Ánte, and the three took to their heels. When they came closer, they could see that, while the high ground was thick with berries, it was so swampy all around, there was no way to get across. The cloudberries were there, but the men couldn't get at them. There was no other choice but to run back to the brush and cut down a couple of birches to use as a bridge. Not exactly something done in a minute.

Finally they could get across. The cloudberries were so thick, there was no place to set their feet down. So they had to pick around the edges first and, in that way, work their way farther and farther into the patch. There were millions of berries, each one as big as a bull's head. It was just a matter of rolling them into the buckets. In no time they had picked sack- and tubfuls and were ready to head for home. They had found the only spot in the entire marsh where there were berries.

This was an experience that Father delighted in remembering, especially when we had trudged around for a long time without any results. Whenever he thought about that great cloudberry trip, fresh light would come into his eyes, and he would gaze about, slowly, searching. But, no matter how hard he looked, with or without the binoculars, the marshes were and continued to be as miserable as ever. He never found a patch like that one again.

From Čáhcegáddái nohká boazobálggis, *1988*
Translated by Edi Thorstensson

John Erling Utsi

The Waves

John Erling Utsi (1952–) is primarily a radio and television journalist, but he has also written short stories for various Sami publications and made children's programs for Sami radio. He lives in Jokkmokk in northern Sweden, a town which has been known for hundreds of years for its Sami Fair, which takes place in February every year. The fair has in recent years also served as a Sami cultural festival, with theatrical performances and yoik concerts. Hordes of people come to this fair, in spite of the fact that it is held during the coldest time of the year, when temperatures can drop to –30 F or even lower. One year, in just such cold, Dálvadis, the Sami theater of Sweden, presented an enactment of a myth on the ice of a lake. The audience sat on reindeer pelts in the snow. During the intermission people could step into Sami teepees called *lavvos*, which were set up on the shore, to warm up with steaming hot reindeer bullion or coffee. The play's stage set consisted of snow and ice. Some years ago, John Erling Utsi wrote an ambitiously conceived play for Dálvadis, which the company took on a tour across Sapmi, traveling from place to place in sleds pulled by reindeer, the traditional means of travel in the old days.

$\mathcal{T}$HE MOUNTAIN LAKE is like an ocean, an open sea without islands. Today the wind is blowing. High waves, white-capped waves splash against the shores, licking sand. They travel higher and higher up onto the land but must reluctantly give up and return to the lake. On their way back, they snatch grains of sand and a few loose rocks and force them to come along, down toward the deep.

As far as the eye can see, there are white waves, and in their wake – more white waves. With shining eyes they wait impatiently, wait for a chance to roll in over the wet shore, to nibble on gravel and sand, to bite and devour.

It's an early autumn morning; the leaves are already yellow, and there's frost at night. The clear air and the cold, southerly gusts of wind pour into people's lungs. The mountain peaks shine white, shine and remind people that winter is on its way.

The night before, Lasse put out the nets as usual. Lasse, the old bachelor of the *siida*, is an avid fisherman. All summer he has pulled up whitefish, this fat, shiny, blind fish that gets caught in his nets at night.

Lasse stands on the sandy shore, looking out over the wind-whipped lake. The gusts are so strong that he constantly has to grab hold of his cap to keep it on. He is looking south, staring into the wind.

"To think that the fall storm would begin this early," he mumbles to himself. "It probably won't quit until the fish are ruined or even rot in the nets."

From the sand bank where he stands looking out over the water, the waves seem like dark green animals. Animals with the souls of bandits. And real bandits they are, the way they have gobbled up the whole narrow headland that used to give the boats such good protection against the wind in the early summer. Now only a couple of little rocks remain. And the waves don't seem to bother about them any more. They roll by them, climb over them, divide into two around them, and continue their journey toward the shore. There, they flow further and further up onto the land, with roaring sounds and cascades of foam.

"Well, I guess I've got to try it, " Lasse says to himself. "If I could only get the boat out a ways before the big waves throw me back ashore."

He puts all his strength into pulling; it's hard work to launch the boat in this weather. The muddy sandbank is long and seems to suck the boat in, unwilling to let go of it.

Lasse has almost managed to get the boat all the way out when his mother comes running.

"You aren't going out on the water in this storm, are you?" she yells, the wind almost drowning her words.

"I can't hear you," answers Lasse.

"I said, you aren't thinking of going out to check the nets in this awful weather? The boat will tip over and that'll be the end of you. Don't kill yourself. Let the miserable fish stay there, even if they get spoiled," she begs.

"If I could just get the boat out a ways, there'd be no problem," Lasse says and tries again.

Just then the wind subsides and everything becomes still, except for the mountains of foam that are breaking against the shore. The waves have such strength, now, that the earth shakes, and the sounds from them are deafening.

Lasse gets the boat into the water, jumps aboard, and grabs an oar to push himself out. Then he lowers the motor and pulls the starter rope. One pull and it starts, and Lasse backs out until he's in deep water.

When he looks toward the shore, he can see his mother. And it seems as if she is wading out into the water after him. The waves are licking the hem of her *gákti*, her cheeks are wet – or could it be tears he sees in her eyes? Lasse doesn't know for sure. It seems as if the waves are trying to trick his mother into going further out, too.

When the boat sinks between two crests, it almost seems as if his mother disappears in the waves, but as soon as the boat is lifted up again, he can see that she is still standing on the shore.

"I'm the one on the lake, not Mother," he thinks.

Then he turns the bow into the wind and speeds away. Now and then a wave comes that is higher than the sandbluffs. White fangs snap at him from its crest. When Lasse sees one of these waves, he jumps up, stops the motor, and angles the boat.

"Am I going to make this one or overturn?"

183

The boat climbs still higher, but just as it's about to heel, it glides down into another valley between the waves. Lasse catches his breath and glances quickly behind him, sees the crest of the waves – cold, greenish-black water.

Beyond them, he discerns the white mountain peaks. They seem so far away – so endlessly far away. Above the peaks he can see a blue sky and a few clouds that are hurrying north.

The waves in the middle of the lake don't seem quite as high. Lasse takes a chance and speeds up. But, suddenly, a gigantic billow comes churning and threatens to capsize the boat. Lasse reacts and stops the engine. The boat climbs to the crest of the billow, and he grows dizzy when he sees how high up he is. Then the boat slides down again, and he doesn't know for sure if what he feels in his stomach is a rush of fear or joy.

Lots of water has sprayed in over the edges of the boat. The bailer is floating around, and it feels as though the boat is butting the waves with increasing frequency. Lasse has no time to bail; he can barely steer and get away from the worst breakers. The gasoline can, too, is floating around in the bottom of the boat. Is it floating because there's so much water, or can it be empty?

The mother is walking up the hill to the *lavvo*. Halfway there, she turns around. But she can't see anything. The wind stirs up the dry sand, blowing it into her eyes, blinding her. All she can do is climb further up, toward the treeline.

Once she is up, she turns her head to look again. The water seems even whiter now than when she was running along the shore below. Only white waves, white as far as she can see. The wind is so strong that the trees bend, these pitiful timberline trees. Birches are rubbing against each other, squeaking and screaming as if in pain.

184

It has been a good many years since she experienced such a fierce storm, she thinks as she stands at her lookout. The other boats of the *siida* lie on the shore, as if they had been scared up there. No one has gone out, no one except for Lasse. The men of the *siida* have done the very opposite; they've pulled their boats further away from the lake, away from the sinister waves.

Nilsa, who lives in the nearest *lavvo*, comes walking along the trail. He has nets out, too. He goes fishing as often as he can. For most of the summer he is in the mountains, where he goes around helping people mark reindeer.

He walks slowly, stopping now and then to look out over the lake. He doesn't know whether to go out or not. He saw Lasse leave and thought of coming along himself, but then his wife came and put her foot down.

He walks up to where Lasse's mother is standing, stops next to her, but neither one of them says anything. They just stand there, looking out.

"That Lasse sure had guts to go out in this storm," Nilsa finally says.

"I couldn't stop him," the mother complains.

A couple of crows fly over. With the wind behind them, they dart by; when they fly into the wind, they hardly move forward from the same spot.

"Can you see his boat?" the mother asks.

"I saw it a while ago, but right now I can't see it. It might be behind Baktesuolu, in which case we can't see it from here."

At the same moment a wind gust hits with such force it almost knocks them off their feet, and they have to step back. The gust stirs up sand from the beach. They can't keep their eyes open and have to turn around and cover their faces.

The mother walks toward the *lavvo*. Deep in thought, she

185

moves slowly on the long, stony path. As she stumbles onward, now and then wiping sand off her face, she thinks about the old days.

I can remember this lake the way it was when I was a little girl and we passed this way in the early summer, on our way north, she thinks. It was so little then and so peaceful, with islands, headlands and bays on its sides. When a storm blew up, we would go up onto one of the islets, make coffee and gather branches to have in the *lavvo*. And if the wind didn't die down, we stayed for the night and thought nothing of it. Everyone in the *siida* moved at the same time. If anyone had already gone ashore on the islet, we stopped, too, even if it was nice and the wind was calm. We went ashore to take a coffee break, repair a motor, fill the motors with gasoline, or just to take a piss. Nobody just went by if someone had already stopped.

In the early summer, the water would be bluish green, not black as it is now. A person couldn't say it was particularly warm, but, at any rate, it looks colder now. At that time, it was as if the lake just lay there and wished people welcome. It doesn't do that anymore. Now it lies there more like a big, terrifying monster, an animal that has had to endure much torture and pain and has gone into hiding here, beneath the mountain, because it can't stand human beings anymore; it probably feels that human beings have caused all its suffering.

And there were birds everywhere when we came to our camp for the summer and went ashore; both sparrows and wading birds, I remember. Sometimes we would even see swans and ducks. Now only the loon remains. The loon with its song of lamentation in the evenings. And there are more crows, wherever they come from, those vulture-like creatures. That's what we have now – the loon with its wailing, and the greedy crow.

The poor mountain lake is like an angry, mean animal that has been injured so severely that it won't put up with any creatures, and it's never going to be like it was before, never.

These were her thoughts as she sat in the *lavvo*, recalling a time that no longer was, remembering both sorrow and happiness. But suddenly she is back in the present. Lasse, she thinks, Lasse is on the lake in the boat! And the wind just keeps getting worse and worse. She is on her knees at the fireplace, looking up through the smoke hole, seeing the clouds drifting northward at a violent speed.

"May God protect him," she whispers in a low voice. She crawls closer to the fire, puts on some more sticks of wood, and hangs the coffee kettle up to boil. Suddenly the wind pushes the smoke back into the *lavvo*, filling the tent with so much smoke she has to lie down on the skins, her eyes burning, her tears flowing.

After a while, the air clears again, and she can see the clouds rushing north, one after the other.

When she gets up, she accidentally touches the clothesline, which has clothes hanging on it to dry, and before she knows it, a sock has ended up in the fire. She rakes it out, but it's too late; there's only a shriveled clump of yarn left of the entire sock.

"Oh no, that I would burn Lasse's sock…"

She kneels in the smoke, tears in her eyes and a half burned-up sock in her hand, pulling and stretching it, but to no avail.

Lasse has caught sight of the first float and tries to pull up beside it, but it disappears under a wave as soon as he approaches. He has to start searching again and find it before he can steer the boat in the right direction.

Just when the float finally is at his side again, it disappears under the boat; he can hear it beating against the boards.

The line had better not get tangled up in the propeller, he thinks. He stops the motor. The boat immediately begins to drift with the wind, and then the float reappears.

Lasse pulls the starter rope and takes aim again.

When he is close enough, he takes the oar and tries to pull in the line with it. He has to stretch far over the gunwale to reach. Suddenly, a breaker surges over him from behind. Lasse has to grab hold of the gunwale and barely manages to avoid being thrown overboard.

"Vuoi, those waves! Blasted storm, damn wind!" he frets and curses.

The waves lick the side of the boat. A few times it's as though they'll devour the boat in one mouthful. One wave is so big it covers the entire horizon, and the mountains disappear behind its white froth. Whenever one of those strikes the bow, it forces the boat higher and higher, and when the boat has reached the crest, the perilous ride down again begins. Then the boat might be rammed by the next wave and forced under.

Lasse defies the waves and tries to get hold of the rope again. He has had a scare, but he is angry, as well. So he carries on.

Nilsa stands at the treeline, staring out across the lake. There are only white-capped waves to be seen. And wind gusts that carry sand from the shoal below, sand that at times blinds him.

He takes no notice of the wind or sand, but stands staring. He begins to think about what happened once the previous summer, another time when the wind was blowing hard out of the south. Lasse and he were out together checking the nets. The wind was so strong that they almost didn't dare go out. He wouldn't have dared to go alone, but Lasse talked him into it, and so they headed out.

When they came to where the nets were placed, the wind had increased. Nilsa wanted to row behind the point and wait for the wind to calm down, but Lasse wanted nothing of such talk. And, as luck would have it, just as Lasse was about to pull up one of the lengths of net, a wind gust came with such force, it almost took him along. And he would probably have fallen overboard if Nilsa hadn't

188

grabbed hold of one of his feet. Lasse had only said, "Hell! I could've become food for the fish there." And then he went on pulling up his nets.

"We were lucky that time," Nilsa mumbles to himself.

Lasse has figured how to get close enough to the floats, and he has already pulled several nets into the boat. There's more fish than he had expected; some of the nets are twisted together into thick ropes by all the fish. He gathers the nets into a heap in the middle of the boat but doesn't take the time to get the fish out. In the end, there's a big pile in the bottom of the boat. The whole jumble of nets in the pile squirms and wriggles and looks alive.

Lasse has only one length of net left, but it's at the roughest part of the whole lake. Smack in the middle of the open water. He has waited to go out there until last, hoping the wind would abate and the waves subside enough to make it possible for him to pull the last nets up.

So far the wind hasn't calmed down, and Lasse is beginning to wonder if it's even worth trying. The waves are skyhigh out there. Everything is completely white.

"Since everything has worked out well so far, I might as well try to get those, too, so I won't regret afterwards that I didn't," Lasse thinks. But he shivers when he sees how the waves are surging further out. The boat is heavy from the nets, the fish, and the water that has gushed in over the gunwale. The gasoline can is still floating around.

Mother has come out of the *lavvo* again and she stands on the hill looking out over the water. The whole lake is like a seething cauldron, but now and then it lies hidden from her view behind the sand that is whipped up from the banks.

189

As she stands there, she catches sight of a crow that is struggling into the wind. But the crow becomes aware of the little woman who stands watching, the hem of her *gákti* and her apron fluttering in the wind. The crow makes a detour past her and lands on the highest *lavvo* pole. The wind comes in sudden squalls, and the crow is barely able to land.

That miserable crow, it just sits there so it can shit onto my hearth, the mother thinks and becomes even more dispirited.

When she glances out over the lake again, she can barely see a dot far from shore. It could be a boat. Around the boat there's only foam.

Is that Lasse, or is it only a rock that the waves are beating against? She runs to the *lavvo* to get her binoculars. The crow, which has settled down in the smoke vent, doesn't get scared when she comes. It sits peacefully on the pole and doesn't have sense enough to fly away.

Lasse is on his way home. In the tailwind, he must be careful so the waves don't come from behind and fill the boat. The load is heavy. Risking his life, he had pulled the last length of net aboard. As he knelt in the boat and pulled, he had to admit that this was insanity, and that he was a big fool.

"Why should I struggle with this slippery whitefish in such ungodly weather? Isn't there a better way to make a living…?"

But he has managed so far, anyway. Now he has the wind at his back. He is on his way home.

Behind him, the waves come rolling, white with foam. It's as though they're snapping at the boat. But they don't reach it, the boat glides away. Higher and higher they rise. When Lasse glances behind him, it looks as if they are going to wash into the boat. But just as they are about to overtake him, they are pushed down by their

190

own weight. With a violent roar and a cascade of froth, they seem to stumble and slow down again.

Then, all of a sudden, the motor begins to sputter. Lasse understands at once what is wrong – he forgot to fill it with gasoline before he set out. He has just had this thought when the motor stops. It becomes quiet, except for the roar of the breaking waves.

The old woman stands there, her binoculars lifted, trying to catch sight of the white spot. But there's nothing for the eyes to see but white-shouldered waves – and blackish green water.

Nilsa comes walking along the trail; it looks as if he is in a hurry.

"Did you hear the motor?" he asks.

"No," she answers. "Have you seen anything?"

"No."

They look at each other, there on the slope of the hill. Mother's eyes shine with fear. In Nilsa's eyes there is mostly astonishment.

The wind sighs and the clouds drift on. A clear autumn sun is shining, unable to warm. Mother wakes up, as if from a dream, and finds herself standing at the edge of the shore, her binoculars in one hand and Lasse's singed wool sock in the other. Sand swirls from the ground, and heavy, dark green waves gnaw at the shore.

From Savvon, *1983*
Translated by Roland Thorstensson

John Gustavsen

"The War Is Over!"

John Gustavsen (1943–) is from Honningsvåg on the Finnmark coast, but he
has been living in Tromsø for a number of years. Honningsvåg has always
been an international place; it is today perhaps best known as the gateway
to North Cape, the northernmost point in Europe, an area which has always
attracted large numbers of tourists. Furthermore, Honningsvåg has always
had the reputation among people in Finnmark of being a "rough" town. For
a time it was called Little Chicago, and that is the title which John
Gustavsen chose for his first collection of short stories, published in 1978.
Gustavsen was a charter member of the Sami Writers' Association and he
has also been a delegate to the European Writers' Congress. He holds a
degree in education but is now primarily a writer of non-fiction, most often
concerning Sami issues, and debate articles on a wide range of topics,
written for periodicals and newspapers.

"**F**ULL SPEED AHEAD! Due north!"

Georg Isaksen shouted and waved his cap to the dozen or so people who were standing on the Bothner-dock in Harstad and longing to go home. The *Lenin*, of Berlevåg, a cutter also called the F45B, was backing out of the harbor, once again loaded full with people and cattle. The *Lenin* was engaged in freight traffic between Harstad and the coast of Finnmark. This time two families were on board, the Juliussens from Honningsvåg and the Ravnas from Lafjord. A miserable time in the Harstad camp had come to an end.

The Ravna family had nine members, counting big and small. They didn't have much with them – a couple of sheep, a sofa, and a few boxes and sacks with odd items in them. During the war they

195

had been called the Ravna pack in the camp. Only the father, Ravna himself, knew a few Norwegian words like *tobakk, margarin* and *hestepølse*, but they had pulled through in spite of it all. They were people of few words. The children had had it rough during the break in the war. One of the boys had gotten his eye poked out, another had lost his hand while playing with enemy explosives.

The Juliussens were part of the "Honningsvågers," a group of people that had been very much in evidence during its stay in Harstad. "They seem to be fighting a war all by themselves," the people of Harstad had said, more afraid of them than of the Germans. Juliussen himself, however, was a terrified-looking little fellow who could never forget the day when the ammunition barge blew up in Honningsvåg, the anchor was sent flying up into the mountains, and cows ran bellowing through the streets, their bowels in tow.

Now Juliussen was going back, too. Georg Isaksen examined the pitiful luggage he had with him: a sofa without legs, a couple of bed-boards, and a few knickknacks.

Just before departure one of the children came leading an emaciated old horse; another child was pulling a cow, so thin it was almost transparent; and a third was being dragged along by a goat. The father of the family was himself pulling a cart with a couple of rowan berry bushes in it.

"Katinka's bringing a forest to Magerøya."

Finally, Katinka herself came waddling along, the dock boards bending under her. The spectators talked among themselves about the seven good years and the seven lean years, but Katinka, paying no attention to them, just bellowed:

"Throw the rope out, and let's get moving!"

The *Lenin* was almost like Noah's ark. The greatest attention was drawn to the figurehead up at the forecastle, Katinka, who had sat down in an armchair and continued with her knitting, unaffected by all the the commotion and hullabaloo.

Aldor Isaksen had been standing by the winch when they loaded cattle and odds and ends. The sheep and the cow were easy enough to load, the goat was stubborn and had bitten one man in the hand, the horse was nervous and skittish.

It wasn't until Katinka roared, "Martyr, be good now!" that the old nag calmed down. Now he just stood there in a big crate, looking rumpled and sad.

"He reminds me of a wooden horse more than anything," Georg said to himself.

Georg and Aldor were at the helm when they left Andfjord. They had made many such trips, could remember many kinds of experiences. Once, when their boat had been overloaded, they were a hair's breadth from being shipwrecked. The westerly wind had gone wild when they were on Lopphavet, the cargo had cut loose and made the boat heel, and a terrified soul wanted to jump overboard. Another person had cheered, but he was a drunkard the war had scared witless.

It could be a real circus to bring people home. It was particularly difficult in Tromsø, because as soon as people got a whiff of *polet*, the liquor store, there was plenty to celebrate. One fellow had emptied the compass on the *Lenin* to get at the alcohol inside. They'd almost run aground in the fog.

"I think we've got peaceful people this time, Pops."

Aldor always called his father "Pops," even though he himself was over thirty-five.

"Yeah. Except for the lady in supreme command; she's like the whole German General Staff we brought over to the *Tirpitz*."

During the war the *Lenin* had been forced into commission by the Nazis for their fleet. Bedridden with tuberculosis, Georg had

197

refused at first. But when the Gestapo agent had fired live ammunition at the wall, and a major had threatened to liquidate the whole family, Georg had given in.

Then the *Lenin* had its name painted over and replaced with the *Bismarck* and became a freighter for everything from butter to oranges and cognac. As it turned out, they had memorable times from the war all the same, from voyages when they had pilfered from the Germans everything from ham and marmalade to ammunition and liquor.

"Aw, we can certainly handle that Katinka."

Georg Isaksen wasn't a person one would joke with, seasoned as he was in fights against greedy local merchants, in battles at sea by Lofoten, and against the invaders.

The *Lenin* was built in Rana in 1934 and lengthened in Korsfjord in Alta in 1938. The cutter was now 54 feet long and 14 feet wide, well over 8 feet deep, and its weight was registered at a gross weight of 24 d.w. tons. Loaded with coal fish, it had once weighed 42 tons, but that was the time the people in Snefjord had yelled:

" Soon it'll be only the beard of that Georg that's above water."

Many wondered how the boat had received its name.

"We've got to have a real name for the boat," was the argument. Georg was known as a Red, eagerly involved in local politics and a member of the Communist party. He had been to Russia several times, and he even spoke a little broken Russian. But he had his baptism by fire when he was fifteen. That was in 1903, when the battle at Svein Foyn's factory out at Mehavn took place. Georg had been there with his father, and he would never forget the guy from Lyngen who had attached the end of the rope to the chimney, and the whole damn thing was going to be reduced to rubble. Those were the days when the working class was cleaning out local tycoons and petty tyrants. Georg was looking forward to the end of the tyranny of the money matadors. He was a man of the color red, only wore his best suit once a year, on May 1. Then he clenched his fist, sang the International, and hoisted the red flag on the *Lenin*. Because he was well-read, he wasn't about to be duped by sweet temptations of the hoity-toity bourgeois world. Therefore he gave no second thought to the question of what to name the boat when it was launched on the anniversary of *Lenin*'s death:

"The *Lenin*."

They were heading toward Senja. There was a light headwind from the northwest. The wind carried the fragrance of birch across the water. There was a faint whistling in the rigging. The atmosphere was serene. But Katinka was barking at her children, while Ellen Ravna, looking slightly scared, was sitting on the hatch to their room, rocking one of her babies. When Aldor had addressed her, she had just answered:

"Not understant Norwegian."

"Aw, she understands when she wants to!" It was Katinka who had spoken. She had comments for everything. And she wasn't particularly fond of the Ravnas.

The Ravnas were part of a Karasjok family, and were going to live in Lafjorden. Georg wondered how they would survive on the little they had, but Aldor knew them better.

"Nah, they don't need much. As soon as their feet are on land again, they'll be moving about at a quicker pace. But I'm more worried about what it's gonna be like in Honningsvåg."

"Yeah, I hear it's a real circus there."

"Aw, it'll work out somehow."

The *Lenin* whipped through Gisundet, with Finnsnes to starboard, and then Gibostad to the port side. Aldor was thinking about the time when a coastal steamer had rammed into the flour storehouse at Gibostad. There hadn't been any snow yet that fall, but that morning the townspeople were awakened by a storm of whirling flour the like of which they had never seen. They thought it was snow. Yes, there sure were all sorts of stories to remember.

Georg had been at the helm for four hours when his son entered the pilothouse.

"How about some fresh coffee?"

"Yeah, it's time for a leak-break anyway."

Georg was a tough fellow at the helm. Could go from Tromsø to Honningsvåg in one stretch, relieved only by a doctored-up cup of coffee and a trip to Siri (the toilet stall). But he had been so tired, a few times, that he had slept when they passed above Lyngen and gone by Loppa. The *Lenin* had made these round-trips so often, it could almost steer itself.

He already saw the jaw of Malangen and caught a glimpse of Kvaløya when he moved forward in the cabin. The warm, sharp smell of coffee came toward him. The bunks were full of children. The Ravna children were as quiet as mice, the Juliussens were like lemmings.

"So you are Impossible-Juliussen's rascals," he bellowed and smiled.

He poured coffee into his mug. It was full of grounds and smelled sour. He liked it that way, took a big gulp and looked at the children.

"Have any of you little trolls fed the crabs?"

"Ingalaila has, she's so sea sick."

"Is she gonna heave?"

"She already has."

"Poor kid."

"She puked in the bed."

"No, in the bunk."

"On the floor, too. Yes, she sure did, but then Georg here will have to swab the floor."

Georg was used to such things, took it with a sense of humor and felt sorry for the children.

"We'll be in Tromsø in a little while, and then the sea will get calmer."

Then he went up. Ravna, who was sitting on the hatch sucking his pipe, was brown-skinned and had dark, sharp beard stubble on his cheeks. He was anything but talkative. Georg said:

"We've been lucky with the weather."

"Yeah".

"You people like the trip?"

"Yoo."

That's how they were, the people from the mountains. Didn't say much.

If Ravna was quiet, Katinka Juliussen was the opposite. She ground her husband like a coffee grinder grinds coffee, and she almost commanded the sea:

"Einar, get me some water!"

"Einar, give me my knitting!"

"Einar, get me some bread!"

"Einar, look after Martyr!"

Georg went up to the pilothouse again. Aldor was standing there with his cap askew, puffing on a hand-rolled cigarette and squinting through the window glass. Toward the east they could see the wild mountains around Malangen. Magnificent snow- and ice-covered peaks against a gray-blue sky. Beneath, a forest of birch trees with new leaves on them. Fields that had just turned green reached down to the sea.

"When're we gonna be in town ?"

"Just before three, if we don't have the current against us."

201

"No, it's with us."

They thundered through Rya at such a speed, the hull was creaking.

"The current runs like a river," Aldor yelled.

"Yeah, you sure can't doze off here."

Shortly thereafter the *Lenin* arrived at the Odd Berg Bridge in Tromsø. Many boats were docked in the harbor. Georg recognized the Finnmark-boats F70 VH, F40 K and many others. People were swarming north these days.

The stopover at Tromsø had to be as brief as possible. Just a few small things had to be taken care of. Oil and water. Provisions. Aldor had to make a stop at the liquor store. It was dangerous to stay too long in town. The bottle enticed many. There was action at every street corner.

It was close to six. The *Lenin* was ready to leave. If only Einar Juliussen would come. They lay with the engine in idle.

"Well, where is that Einar, Katinka?"

"Are you asking me?" Katinka looked puzzled. "He's found bad company, I guess, and is hittin' the bottle."

Half an hour went by, then a whole one. The children were becoming anxious.

"Wonder if he's fallen into the sea, Mother?"

"Then he's so drunk he'll float, sure enough."

"Where can he be?"

"Where there's booze."

Aldor and Georg looked at each other, because this was nothing new to them. Tromsø was like flypaper. People got stuck there. They were mighty thirsty after the long war, and the doors to *polet* were wide open. Some people spent all their money there. Aldor often had to go ashore and hunt for people. He jumped up on the dock.

"I'll take a walk up the street."

"Just look where they sell beer." Katinka had no doubts. "That lush is hiding in a bar, no doubt about it."

Aldor moseyed around from one place to another. No Einar.

"So, you didn't find the rascal." Katinka was red in the face, visibly incensed.

"Oh, he's probably just around the corner." The last words he said to dampen the rage of the one in the arm chair. She was now knitting up a storm. Close to an hour went by. Then one of the children cried out:

"Here comes Dad!"

A man on happy legs had just come around the corner of the warehouse, sailing over the dock boards with a paper bag in his hand, waving his arms frantically, singing and babbling:

"Tjo å hei, hoppsasay
Now the Germans have gone away
tjo å hei ramtatay
now Strong-Einar is so gay."

Katinka had gotten fired up, just like an old steam engine. Her eyes were like lightening bolts as Aldor helped her animated husband aboard.

"He's gonna get a thrashing!"

"Just wait 'till I get you to myself, you lout."

"Well – hick – what's my little rosebud saying… ain't she sweet as honey?"

Einar Juliussen was in rare form when the *Lenin* set out from the dock. But Katinka was ready with her sentence:

"Throw that drunken swine down into the cabin, unbutton his pants, and he's gonna get some real treatment."

203

Aldor had already pulled the ropes aboard. Ravna, light as the wind, had dashed up on the dock and cast off. Georg and Aldor were at the helm.

"Let's have one for the town."

"Yeah, I think we've earned that."

They remained standing there, talking to each other. Georg had heard the weather forecast. It was bad. He took a big swig from the bottle.

"We'll be warm enough now, Aldor," he said and smiled in his beard.

Georg was known for being careful with liquor. Aldor could certainly get sloshed now and then, but Georg was always in full control. The waves alone provided enough rocking aboard the ship. Georg had received invaluable training. He had watched the tactics used by many of the local merchants. Several of his own companions had allowed themselves to drink until they were easily duped. Some had drowned in bottomless debt to the merchants. All too many had been fooled out of both gear and boat. The merchants charged outrageous prices for their merchandise and paid shamefully little for the fish. Georg had often discussed this with his son.

Toward the evening they passed Ullsfjorden. Georg was alone at the helm. Aldor was napping in the cabin. The wind was getting stiffer, and the rigging was booming. He felt the hull beating against the waves and heard the horse neigh. Through the porthole he saw dark, red clouds in the northwest. At Kvænangen they could easily get breakers to struggle against.

The atmosphere in the main cabin was explosive. Ten children and four grownups had made it their home. Two languages were spoken. Einar Juliussen lay snoring on one of the benches. Katinka Juliussen sat at the stove and stoked it up so vehemently that the rings almost took to the air. Sweat was oozing from her. She was happy to be heading north.

Katinka Juliussen was one mean worker, never idle. She was strict, but fair. And religious. But she did swear.

"Mother, you're so mean," Kajsa would say.

"I've got to keep you all in check, by God, especially that father of yours."

She looked over at her husband. She was actually quite fond of him, but – what a little wretch he was. What would've happened to them if she hadn't taken on extra work? She had baited fishing lines, baked rolls, and knitted socks. There'd sure be some rough times when they got home. Honningsvåg had become a wild place, she had heard. Those were the rumors that had traveled south to them a long time ago. She looked at the man; how would she be able to keep him away from the bottle?

Elias Ravna sat on the bench, sucking his pipe. His flock of children and his wife were all piled up on a bunk up front in the cabin. He himself was looking forward to coming back to Lafjorden. The Germans had burned down people's houses, but they had let their turf huts stand. The Germans may have felt that people couldn't live in such things, anyway. Elias was thinking about all they had to do when they got back. But they did have something to fall back on, didn't they? The lakes and the streams would be full of fish; besides, they could catch hares and ptarmigan. And this would be a good year for berries. They had the sea, too, the blessed Lafjorden. They knew every bump of the fjord bottom, and every shallow area. Ellen and he had fished so much in the fjord before the war that the drying racks for drying fish had almost fallen down.

He sucked his pipe and smiled to himself. They had children and children meant happiness. They followed nature's course.

Elias hadn't liked it in Harstad. Neither had Ellen. Just trouble there. "Norwegians not much better than the Germans," he had said one day. People caroused and fought, and that wasn't anything for him. He had shod horses during their stay, and Ellen had given birth to a couple of children. He dreamt about coming home to Skuotannjarga.

Elias gave a sudden start when he noticed how the *Lenin* was pounding against the waves. Oh yeah, they'd make it for sure. He looked over at the stove, at the mighty woman. She looked fearsome. "A lot of woman in one embrace," he mused to himself.

Aldor woke up around nine in the evening, rubbed his eyes, got dressed, and scurried up to the poop deck. A strong wind was coming straight toward him. The horse, he thought, and he gathered some wisps of hay and filled a bucket with fresh water. Martyr looked as if he had trudged up a bunch of hills, but he recovered when he got a little care. Aldor stroked him and said a few nice words. Then he moved slowly up to his father in the pilothouse. Georg was at the helm, half asleep.

"The wind has gotten nasty."

"Have you heard the forecast?"

"It's not even ten yet, Pops." His father looked a bit dazed.

"Want me to take over?"

"Yeah, I'd better go and listen to the weather god." The father went back to the instrument panel and put his ear to the radio receiver. The reception was miserable out here between the massive mountain walls, but the voice of the weather man in Tromsø penetrated through the noise and static.

"Moderate gale during the night," Georg grumbled to his son.

"Then it'll be impossible at Loppa."

"Yes, but I think we could try to get out at Kvænangen. If it gets too damn mean, we'll have to go up to Andsnes."

"Yeah, we can cast anchor in the lee of Loppa if the wind gets completely out of control."

"It stirs up a lot of waves when it comes from that direction."

"But we could slip in to Sandland or Bergsfjor'n – and then we can get some lamb meat from Evald."

"You're thinking about that old flame of yours, aren't you?"

The father was joking. Aldor had run around with a girl from Bergsfjord during his bachelor days. But that love affair had evaporated when he found a first class woman in Tromsø.

They rocked their way out of Kvænangen. The waves came toward them head-on, gushing in over the deck.

"The horse is the worst off."

"But we sure tied him up, didn't we?"

"Yeah, it'll be one big tangle if the box breaks loose."

"Yeah, do you remember when we had to put Fridtjof at Veidsnes's mare out of its misery?"

"God, yes! Animals are dangerous cargo, that's for sure."

The *Lenin* took the high waters well, a splendid sea boat. It would be worse when the wind came from the side, not to mention when it came from the quarter side. Father and son worked together when the weather was like this.

At about two in the morning they sailed around Brynilen, the border between Troms and Finnmark. The point was jutting out into the sea like a knife.

"I think there's a heavy gale out at sea." Georg Isaksen was adept at reading weather and wind conditions. He had gone through both full gale and shipwreck on the banks of North Cape and looked death in the eye more than once. A mighty man of the sea. That he was getting uneasy now was mainly because of the young cattle and the children. In a brief flash he got to thinking of Katinka's "forest", and that made him smile. But he felt he had to go and look after the ant hill in the cabin, and he told Aldor so.

The moment he opened the deckhouse, the foul odor of vomit hit him. He climbed down the ladder. Just what he had thought: the children had vomited, even on the bedclothes. Katinka, who had been sitting with her head over the bucket, looked up as he climbed down.

"Are you trying to kill us all?"

He didn't respond. Knew full well this wasn't a very humane way to transport people, but he wasn't ready for any sarcastic remarks. The group looked slightly unconscious, and he quickly climbed up again.

"We have to get to a port as soon as possible, Aldor. The whole lot's exhausted. The cabin smells like the fish liver barrels that used to stand by the warehouse in Harstad."

"Yeah, we'll have to run before the wind into Bergsfjorden. Then we can take the course through Stjern Sound tomorrow."

The *Lenin* pounded its way through the storm. Aldor went down and checked the engine. A Brunvoll, 50 horsepower. He knew it well, talked to it and greased the bearings. Good engine, never a problem.

After an hour's tumbling about, they changed their course and pulled landward by Silda. The boat took the heavy waters from the back beautifully. From the pilothouse they could see the clouds chase through the air. In the middle of the stormy night, they held their course just beneath Sandland. The war had ravaged here, too. Georg clenched his fist when he thought of all the atrocities the Nazis had committed here. Thought of the war years and the people who had to bleed while the big wheels got fattened up.

The *Lenin* waltzed into the fjord in favorable wind. They caught a glimpse of the Svartfjell glacier, 3,500 feet up. Under it lay Bergsfjord. The boat floated lightly on the crests of the waves. It was exactly six o'clock in the morning when they let the anchor drop. Georg straightened up, felt weak-kneed and tired. Said nothing. Now it would be nice with a couple of hours' sleep. Then he'd see what the new day had in store for them.

In the front of cabin, many of them woke up when the chain rumbled into the water. Einar Juliussen came to with a head-splitting hangover.

"What, already home?"

No answer. He asked the question again, but Elias Ravna just shook his head before he put on his tanned hide boots and dashed up to the deck with a bucket full of vomit. He livened up when he felt the fresh sea air.

"What, isn't this Persfjor'n?"

"This is Bergsfjorn, all right," Aldor answered him. "Tell the others to settle down and get some sleep."

As soon as the *Lenin* had calmed down and Aldor had stopped the engine, Georg slipped down to his cabin. There it was always nice and quiet. Heat from the engine room seeped in. Above the table hung two pictures, one of Jesus and one of Lenin, born 1870, died 1924. Georg snapped his fingers to cheer himself up a little bit. Talked to Lenin, greeted him:

"Spakåjna, nåtsji. Da fstretsji."

"Åtsjin' prijatna."

He greeted, asked how things were going. Well, not too bad.

"Spasiba kharasjå," answered Lenin.

Some Russian phrases had stayed with him since the time of the coastal Pomor trade. He remembered the coastal inhabitants to the east, the terrible poverty he had seen there, but also the friendship he had encountered.

Weary and hungry, he crawled under the bed covers, dressed only in his woolen underwear. Thought of the Russians who had helped in the liberation of Finnmark.

In the cabin there was a lot of commotion. The children were awake, in miserable condition. They were all busy cleaning up the worst of

209

the vomit. Aldor and Einar carried water, while Katinka and Ellen scrubbed the cabin floor. Ellen also ran up and shook the bed covers, wrinkling her nose.

"Vuoi, foul."

Einar and Elias started lowering the sharp-sterned little boat. When the boat hit the water's surface, Einar jumped overboard. A bag of empty bottles was handed down to him. Now he'd go ashore and get some milk and perhaps some meat.

Elias rowed vigorously into the bay. The *Lenin* looked like a bird on the water.

The boat touched the shore, and he pulled it up a little bit. If he wasn't mistaken, a family from Kautokeino lived there. The Buljos, he thought. If they did, he could get meat, perhaps some marrow bone. Vuoi, that was a long time ago...

He strolled up to one of the huts. A man in reindeer hide boots approached him. They greeted each other in the Sami manner.

"Buorre idit."

"Ipmel atti."

They remained standing and talked. Einar noticed the eyes of a child in the hut. Sure enough, here he got both meat and milk.

On the *Lenin*, the children were having a fight over a fishing line. Aldor had to untangle them and find another line so that each of the two families could fish a little. After a few minutes, cod fish and a couple of small halibut lay on the deck.

"A lot of pike here!" yelled one of the children.

"The red one looks like a troll brat."

"That's enough now!" It was Katinka who put a stop to it all before the deck was full. Aldor cleaned the fish and hung some of them up to dry.

When Elias returned, there was a lot of commotion. Not only did he have three bottles of milk with him but also a leg of reindeer. Now they could eat. He smiled and started cutting the meat up. Plates were set on the table, old newspapers spread out.

It was close to one o'clock when Aldor went to wake his father. Georg woke up and turned around:

"How's the wind?"

"It has calmed down. There's coffee and food."

"Yeah, I heard my stomach rumble," said the father and jumped out of the bunk. He was a spry 60-year-old with sharp, piercing eyes.

Close to twelve the *Lenin* moved slowly out of Bergsfjorden. The sea was still choppy, so it didn't take them long to agree on taking the interior course: Stjern Sound – Varg Sound – Kval Sound – Sammel Sound. It would take them an hour longer, but it would mean less work.

"We won't be in Honningsvåg until midnight."

"We'll have to go over to Lafjorden first, you know."

There weren't as many signs of summer in Finnmark as in Troms yet. The fields, the mountains, the meadows – everything showed that. They knew these waters, every point and every mountain peak. Now the landscape was stripped, there were only ruins to behold. The war had ravaged the land severely. In some places people were in motion. The nation was getting on its feet again.

Havøysund was a sad sight. Here people had started up again, too. Georg recognized a lot of boats. He had fished together with the Havøysund people, knew them as an enterprising bunch. Here was Johannes Olsen's boat. True, Johannes was a sly sort of a fellow, a man of the Labor Party. Georg couldn't think much about politics now, he didn't have the energy. Sure, the Labor Party was

211

supposed to fight for the little guy. The future would, of course, tell, but Georg had his own thoughts. He was of the old school.

They passed Måsøy. Georg recognized the local merchant's boat, cutting across the fjord. He remembered many encounters with him, and the time people from Honningsvåg stripped his cloudberry bog. "If he had only known, the devil," he thought.

It was close to midnight when they cast anchor at Lafjorden. A rowboat appeared. Elias and Aldor lowered the sharp-sterned boat. Now it was just a matter of getting everything ashore. Rasmus, a relative of the Ravnas, appears. A dark-skinned man with a cigarette butt between his lips.

"Makkár vanas dat lea?"

Elias answered in Sami and mentioned the *Lenin*. The two kept talking, but Aldor didn't understand a word.

"Speak Norwegian!" Katinka commanded. But Rasmus babbled on, spat through the side of his mouth, pulled children into the rowboat, one after the other.

They began rowing in the direction of the shore.

"Look at that crow's nest!" Katinka exclaimed.

Elias rowed the two sheep and the bags ashore. The sheep were as wild as could be and jumped overboard. There was pandemonium before they reached the shore. Dogs were barking, people were screaming and waving. Smoke was rising from a turf hut.

Georg had navigated the *Lenin* as close to the shore as possible. He could see the bottom through the water, which was crystal-clear. He saw codfish swimming above the seaweed and halibut loafing over the sand. There was a lot to live on in Lafjorden.

The Ravna-people had reached their destination. Georg observed that Finnmark was in the process of waking up. They bid farewell to the people of the fjord, the people of the mountains.

The sea was calm now. Magerøya shimmered green in the light

212

from the midnight sun. Familiar areas of the mountains became visible. The horizon was not to be mistaken. Katinka was sitting on the forecastle, mightier than ever. She had spread a wool blanket over herself and was knitting up a storm.

The Juliussens were going to live in God's house, the only one the Germans had spared. In the church there were all kinds of people: bakers, fishermen, teachers. Some were praying, others cursing.

Honningsvåg was unrecognizable.

"God, what a battlefield," Katinka remarked.

A few barracks were put up, but more than anything they looked like ruins. When the *Lenin* touched the temporary dock, a tear fell from Katinka's eye. There were a lot of people on the dock, even children, although it was in the middle of the night. Some were waving, others were clapping their hands, a few were laughing.

Katinka Juliussen was the first one to drag herself up onto the dock, motherly and grand. Many are those who remember her first words:

"The war is over!"

From Lille Chicago, *1978*
Translated by Roland and Martin Thorstensson

Ellen Marie Vars

Boarding School

Ellen Marie Vars (1957–) is from Láhpoluoppal, in the middle of Finnmark's high plateau or tundra land. She is both an author and a journalist. Her novel *Kátjá*, written for young people and published in 1986, was the first novel written by a woman in the Sami language. She has since published three more books for young readers, the most recent in 1996, and two children's books. She is also represented in a collection of poetry written by three women. At present, Vars serves as editor for a Sami newspaper published in Guovdageaidnu/Kautokeino.

*T*HE FIRST DAY AT SCHOOL and the days that followed were all alike. Kátjá quickly learned what it was like to live at the boarding school and attend classes. She didn't understand why no one was supposed to talk about their parents or home, but that was the message she got on the very first evening, when she explained where she was from. The two girls who came over to her looked friendly.

"What's your name, and where are you from?" they asked. Kátjá was eager to answer. She told them about her family back home and about her grandmother.

"Do you have reindeer?" asked the girls.

"No, we don't. We have cows and sheep," Kátjá answered quietly.

217

The girls sneered. Then one of them kicked her and said, "Then how come you walk around in a *gákti*? You're not Sami if you don't have reindeer. All Sami kids have reindeer. You can't live at this boarding school, only Sami kids get to live here!"

They struck at Kátjá and drove her out of the school. Crying, Kátjá ran away, toward town. On the way she met some children on bicycles. They weren't wearing gáktis. One of them pointed at her and yelled something insulting, but Kátjá didn't understand, because it was in Norwegian.

The others laughed and mimicked the way the Sami speak Norwegian. They pushed their bicycles threateningly at Kátjá, who became so frightened that she turned and ran back toward the school. But they caught up with her, tore off her cap, and threw it in the ditch.

She didn't dare retrieve it, she just ran away as fast as she could. Scared to death, she looked desperately for a place to hide at the boarding school. She saw a cabinet in a corner, standing a bit away from the wall. She squeezed herself behind it, closed her eyes tightly, and pressed her hand over her mouth, so no one would hear her cry.

"If I close my eyes tightly enough, maybe I'll be with Grandma," she thought. Grandma! It was a long time before she dared move. Finally, she couldn't stand to stay squeezed behind the cabinet any longer. Cautiously she crept out, looked around, listened and waited. The coast was clear. She quickly sneaked out to look for her cap. There it lay, at the edge of the road, embedded with sticky clay. She dashed back, found a bathroom in the school, and began to scrub her cap. Most of the dirt disappeared, but the lump in her throat remained.

Days, evenings, and nights were equally horrible. Kátjá was always hungry, but she couldn't get herself to eat. She just cried. None of the grownups, not even the teacher, asked her why she cried so much. Nor did they concern themselves with the fact that the other children hit her, even though they often saw it happen. The children hit and kicked her and pulled her hair, but the adults didn't do a thing to stop them. Before long, Kátjá hated all the grownups and the migrant Sami children, who picked on her the most. Picked on her because her parents didn't own reindeer.

"You're poor," they teased. "People who don't have reindeer are just poor trash."

She had no friends, but then she didn't feel like playing with anyone, anyway, because she was so homesick. Her body ached all the time, too, but it was the homesickness that hurt the most. The mere thought of Grandmother brought tears to her eyes, even in the classroom. But Grandmother was far away.

"If I only knew the way home, I'd run away now!" Kátjá often thought during class time.

The first snow fell, but it didn't cheer Kátjá up. Back home, this was always a big event. Grandmother used to wake her up early with a secretive whisper, "Look out the window, little helper!"

And Kátjá would run to the window before she was fully awake. Her sleepiness vanished when she saw the pure, white snow. It was always so nice! Afterwards, she would cozy up to Grandmother again.

But here, at the boarding school, there was no one who cared about Grandma or the new snow. One day, when the air was thick with snow, Biret came up to her and said that Father would come in two days to bring them home for Christmas.

Home! To Grandmother. Tears began to run down her cheeks, and her heart pounded. Grandma!

When she arrived home, she threw herself onto Grandmother's lap and sobbed so that her entire little body shook. She clung to Grandmother. It was as though she no longer had any words, only tears.

Grandmother stroked her face and spoke to her lovingly.

Kátjá cried for the longest time, until she fell asleep in Grandmother's lap. Grandmother carried her to bed.

"Can school be good for Sami children?" she sighed. Her eyes were full of sadness as she looked at her little helpmate, lying there asleep. "Poor little thing. I wonder what you have been through. And this is just the beginning!" She sat a long time beside the sleeping child.

She remembered the night when Kátjá was born during terrible weather. Was that a sign that hers would be a stormy life?

"Dear Lord, please give her the strength to make it through!"

The long, sad winter finally ended. The sun shone behind the pale clouds, and with the sun there was spring in the air.

But, for Kátjá, it didn't feel like spring. She couldn't hear or smell spring's arrival while she was in school. She often thought about that as she stared out the window during the endless afternoons after classes.

"Why is the spring sun so strange and cold here? Back home it's so warm. I'll bet it has melted some of the snow already. At least enough so that Father can find dry ground for his campfire, and he can boil coffee when he's out duck hunting. I wonder if he has gotten many birds this year. What if my little brother is big enough now to run out and meet Father when he comes home from duck hunting? Maybe he's even learned the names for all the different kinds of birds. I wonder if Father misses me when I'm not around to ask what happened on his hunting trip. Mother probably doesn't have time to ask which birds have already arrived. And Grandma doesn't need to ask Father about anything. She already knows everything.

"Oh, how I wish I could watch when the ice breaks up! Go along with Mother and Father when they put the boat in the water. Row between the ice floes. That used to be so much fun!"

220

When the ice broke up, they went out and set the nets. Father always brought along the shotgun on trips like that. He could hear the ducks long before they came near. He would quickly fasten the net to the boat and get out his shotgun. Kátjá used to duck down in the front of the boat and wait anxiously. You could hear the long-tails a mile away. They flew in flocks and made a big racket. The common scoters would show up suddenly, only two or three at a time. She had never really figured out how they made that pretty whistling sound when they flew. What if Father had gotten a wild goose! How she longed to be along on a duck hunting trip. Just think of coming home with all the birds Father had shot and proudly showing them to Grandma!

The food at the boarding school seemed even more unappetizing when she thought about fresh roast duck.

But spring brought summer, and Kátjá's first year at school finally came to an end.

It was strange to come back to the familiar tundra. As soon as the school bus pulled up, they could see Father sitting there, a ways away, boiling coffee. Kátjá felt that she had come home.

She ran to him. Her feet felt so light. Father! Father!

He stood up and lifted her up onto his shoulders, saying, "Why, honey, you don't weigh a thing! How thin you've gotten. Here, first you have to eat some of this jerky, so you'll have the strength to walk home."

But Kátjá couldn't calm down enough to sit and eat. She had to run around, for she had suddenly become so light. It was almost as though she were flying.

The walk home was as in a dream. Kátjá walked ahead of the others along the crooked path, anxious to see whether they would be home soon. When Father stopped at their usual resting place, she didn't have the least interest in taking a break. It took the others, all of whom had things to carry, such a long time to eat and rest.

When they came closer to home, they began to trot. Even Biret, who had the most to carry. Kátjá saw Grandmother standing there, in the distance. She had come to meet them!

"Grandma!"

Kátjá set off running toward her. The path disappeared in a mist of tears, and she stumbled. She got up quickly and ran on. Grandmother almost toppled over when Kátjá threw herself around her neck.

"Grandma, you smell so good." Kátjá cried as she spoke.

"Little helper, how pale you are. Don't you eat anything at school?"

Kátjá didn't answer, she just kept her arms around Grand-mother, afraid that the old woman might disappear if she let go. The others caught up, and they continued on toward the house. Grand-mother told about everything that had happened while they were away. Kátjá's little brother was a big boy now, good at helping. The cat had had kittens, and in the barn were three new calves, and Father had bought a new boat and net. A big boat with plenty of room for fish.

Grandmother hadn't heard the cuckoo yet, which she thought was odd. Kátjá stopped. "Look, Grandmother, the trees here have already begun to turn green, but at school they are just dark and ugly."

Only when they had come inside, and Kátjá had eaten all she wanted, did she realize how tired out she was.

She asked Grandmother to lie down with her on the reindeer skin in the corner of the room and tell some more about everything that had happened while she had been away at school. Grandmother told about the spring flood and about all the fishing and hunting trips. She kept on talking, long after Kátjá had been lulled to sleep by her warm voice.

Kátjá opened her eyes, surprised. Was she still dreaming? She saw the little room at home and heard familiar voices! She quickly closed her eyes again, in order to hold onto her dream. She lay quite still. Slowly, a feeling of happiness came over her. She was home! Kátjá got up and ran to the kitchen. Gone were the school and all the hardships she had endured. She sat down on Mother's lap, ravenous once again. It was lovely to be home again, just like before, and to eat Mother's good food. Mother and Father asked about school, but Kátjá didn't answer. It was just too painful to think or talk about. She couldn't find words terrible enough to describe the school. Kátjá kept on eating in silence. Ate and ate, as though she hadn't tasted food in years! At last she felt full. She couldn't stand to sit inside any longer. She had to see absolutely everything! First, the new boat. Wow, so big! It has to be the biggest boat in the whole world. There must be room for hundreds and hundreds – no, thousands and thousands of fish!

She hopped and jumped across the meadow, filled with bubbly joy. It was so good to just run, free of pain and hardship, with no fear of being beaten up or teased!

Suddenly she stopped. There was the cuckoo! She stood completely still, listening. Then she began to run. She had to tell Grandma that the cuckoo had come! Grandma, who always says that summer is really on its way when the cuckoo calls.

Kátjá played with her little brother, Joavnna. She went and got pieces of wood from the shed to represent the teacher and the housemother.

"The housemother is a strange lady who always says that I'm dirty. She talks really funny, and she smells funny, too," Kátjá explained. Her little brother listened, round-eyed.

223

"The housemother never answers when I ask her anything, and she doesn't care when the big kids hit the little ones. She is really stupid." Kátjá hit the "housemother" log with a twig. Joavnna helped. They hit and pounded for all they were worth. It was fun to give the stupid housemother a good beating.

"The teacher is an idiot, too," said Kátjá. "She never says a word to the other kids when they make fun of me because I can't speak Norwegian. The teacher doesn't understand a thing, so she gets a beating, too!"

Kátjá and her little brother punished the housemother and teacher for quite a while. It was good for the stupid women to get a sound beating. They deserved to suffer, too. Joavnna heard all about the Norwegians; that it was people like that whom all children had to fear and obey, because if they didn't, they got their ears pinched and were sent to stand in the corner. "At school it isn't allowed to talk about your family or home, and in the boarding house you have to fight all the time," Kátjá continued. "You have to watch out, otherwise you get a beating or your clothes get spoiled." Her little brother's eyes grew dark with indignation. "They laugh because Grandma can't speak a word of Norwegian, and because Mother and Father don't have reindeer, they just have gáktis."

They sat talking like this for a long time. Joavnna understood that the school was a bad place, and he promised that, when he started to go there, he would flatten the whole lot of them if they so much as came near Kátjá.

The summer went quickly, and the time for school to begin approached. All summer, Kátjá brooded over how she would manage to stand another year. She and her little brother came to the conclusion that a person had to be really mean in order to survive at the school. Kátjá decided that no one would get the chance to beat her up again. All summer, she and her little brother practiced fighting.

But she had a stomach ache for several days before school began, because she worried so much. On her last night at home, she clung to Grandmother. When morning arrived, she begged Grandmother to come along with her to school. But Grandmother couldn't, and Kátjá had to leave the warmth and safety of her grandmother and family. She followed reluctantly behind Father and the others.

The school year went all right, in a way. Each day was as dismal and long as the one before, with nothing to especially enjoy. Kátjá taught herself to be as hard as a rock, just in order to survive at the boarding school. Never again did she cry when others could see her; but not a single, long night went by without her pillow's being wet.

She would never depend on anyone again, either, never tell anyone about herself, never expose her feelings.

Here a person ate at mealtimes, even if they weren't hungry. When a person really was hungry, there was no food to be had between meals. Everything she had learned at home should not be done, she had to do at school and in the boarding house.

Life at the school was the opposite of home. She had to force herself to put up with it all. She got to feel in earnest what it means to not be a migratory Sami child.

"You are nothing," said the children of reindeer owners. "Don't think you are Sami, because you aren't," she heard every day at the boarding house. At school she was made to see that she wasn't Norwegian, either, that she didn't have Norwegian clothes. The kids at church pestered her constantly.

Kátjá couldn't understand why it had to be this way, why they thought she was so different. She soon began to hate them because she couldn't understand. She was filled with hate toward everyone

225

and everything that had anything to do with school. Her hatred made her unafraid, dangerous. She could fight; she no longer feared anyone. Even the biggest children grew wary of her when they discovered how diabolically naughty she had become. She was small but quick and strong, and she despised everyone. She couldn't care less about the housemother; stuck out her tongue and spoke nothing but Sami, so the woman didn't understand a word. The other children approached her with caution, suddenly wanting to be friends with Kátjá, who was so good at fighting. But she didn't want to be anyone's friend. She just wanted to be left alone.

Kátjá stopped smiling. She kept to herself, and she was left alone. No one teased her, no one hurt her, and no one dared fight with her any more.

From Kátjá, *1988*
Translated by Edi Thorstensson

Inger-Haldis Halvari

Little Lake, Hear Me!

Inger Haldis Halvari (1952–) has distinguished herself above all as an author of children's books, but she has published a number of short stories as well. She is a native of Polmak in Deatnu/Tana, close to the Finnish border. Halvari has devoted herself to exploring the opposite poles of life: how a child comes into being, on the one hand, and how a child reacts to the loss of an immediate family member, on the other. In her first book, published in 1982, *Dalle go áddjá jámii* [When Grandfather Died], the theme is a grandfather's death and how the book's young protagonist works through her grief. In the selected short story presented here, childhood and feelings of loss are once again important ingredients.

HERE ARE SO MANY DISTURBING SOUNDS this Saturday night, or any other night, for that matter. Cars and motorcycles drive back and forth on the street. All kinds of voices blend with the sound of engines. A boat announces its arrival. Ánne has just gotten the baby to sleep. When she hears the boat whistle, she runs to the window, looks at the clock. Oh, here comes the boat from back home. What if it is bringing me visitors!

She looks out, knowing full well that they don't expect company now. But can a person be so sure? She listens. There are sounds outside, sounds inside. Above her, below her, there are people everywhere.

229

But she is so alone. She bursts out: "Damn it. Damn it, anyway! I wish I could speak to someone else, just one single word. I wonder what Biera is doing now."

She goes from window to window, stops in front of the mirror.

"Wedding present!" She turns up her nose at her own image.

"I'll do it. It's now or never."

Slowly, Ánne begins to undress. Takes off the sweater that the baby has spat up on. Takes off her slacks and socks. In this prison of sounds and walls, Ánne stands naked before the mirror.

"Wedding present," she says through her teeth.

"I am giving you two this mirror, so that you, Biera, will have a good-looking wife for a long time. The mirror always tells the truth."

This was the congratulations that Biera's uncle had come up with. And, judging by the way the wedding guests had laughed, maybe some of them were still laughing.

The mirror doesn't lie!

Ánne puts her hands in front of her eyes, clenches her teeth, tightens all her muscles. When she lowers her hands, she sees her heavy breasts with their stretch marks. Her nipples are red and sore. The baby sure sucks hard. Or is there something wrong with me?

Ánna strokes her nipples carefully, but they are so terribly painful. She has never had breasts like her friends'. Theirs were nice, upturned. Hers were like two lumps of well-risen bread dough! She had always been ashamed and tried to hide them. Once a boy had yelled after her, "You old cow!"

Ánne turns around in front of the mirror. Sees her round body. Presses her belly, takes handfuls of loose, quivering flesh. She feels and sees! The mirror doesn't lie, it tells that she has had a child. Only four weeks have passed since she carried the baby under her heart. It was all right to be round then.

230

Raindrops begin to splash. Ánne stands, paralyzed, in front of the mirror. A scream forces itself from her. Far away, she hears an old cow coming closer and closer. Ánne has seen it for a long time. It's udder and belly droop, it's thighs are like mountains. Again she clenches her teeth, trying not to howl. Even the passing cars seem to call out to good-looking women.

Biera surely remembers his uncle's words. That's exactly why he has gone out now, to find a pretty girl he can sit next to... lie beside, caress, kiss. Poor Biera has had so many exams to take, he needs to get out and meet other people. Everybody has a right to go out on the town and have a beer.

"See other people!"

I am a nobody, an old cow. Whenever my tits are ready to burst, the milk just pours out, and the baby has to nurse. If "poor, tired" Biera would just come home, I'd give him an earful.

I want to go north, where you are, deep, dark little lake. When the boat comes in tomorrow, I'll be standing on the dock with the child I've brought into the world. Someday, she'll probably have to wait for a tired husband, too.

Ánne sinks down on the pile of clothes at her feet. She paws at the floor with her hands and cries, "You are so far away, my little lake, I can't reach you, I can't reach.... Can't reach."

When her sobs ease a bit, she sits back and whispers, "Little lake, you have drawn me to you since my childhood, whenever I was alone, whenever poisonous snakes found their way into my schoolwork."

Ánne stops and sighs. Her eyes are swollen, her throat sore.

"Little lake, if only I could come to you. I've stored up so much that you could have helped me with. There are thousands of people here, but they just rush off, their eyes always look straight ahead.

"Little lake, please hear me!"

231

I'm in such pain, I'm so alone. The worst was the other night. I took care of the little one at midnight. Biera was awake, too. He didn't like that the baby was crying. So I held her and walked around, so he could get some rest. I do that at night, you see.

But first I have to tell you about something that made me happy. Last evening Biera bathed the baby for the first time. Oh, that warmed my heart so. It was so good to hear Biera talk to her.

Biera's eyes shone, and I thought, "I love you so."

Biera sat down with us, we were three. The father's strong hand stroked his child's head, the husband's hand stroked his wife's bare shoulder. All my pain vanished. I was up north, under the birch tree, and the moss I was sitting on was so soft. The summer wind rocked us. And my love was as deep as you. Love had many depths.

We slept so peacefully. When the baby woke up again, I was still full of happiness. It didn't seem so hard to change the baby. I quickly got back into bed to nurse her. Biera had woke up. He watched me and smiled warmly. I could have begun to yoik right there, in the middle of the night, but I didn't dare. Biera would have asked me to stop. He didn't like my songs. He said they belong to the past.

I didn't want my joy to end there. The baby who was no longer just mine sucked at my breast. Biera lay behind us. Two warm hands grasped me. He was so close to me. His body was full of fire.

Nothing was as good as his warm, firm body. I wasn't just a dishwasher, after all. I nursed the baby, our little one. On my back I felt his breath, he needed me, wanted me.

I said, affectionately, "Biera, wait just a minute, don't rush me so!"

But he didn't have time to wait. Before my body could follow his up love's steep hills, he came and was done, and I was never allowed, my little lake, to feel you hold me in your depths.

From Sápmi, *1986*
Translated by Edi Thorstensson

Aagot Vinterbo-Hohr

Palimpsest

Aagot Vinterbo-Hohr (1936–) was born in Snefjord, Finnmark. She lived for a long time in Austria, where she was trained as a physician. She has received research grants in medicine and also had practices in several places in Finnmark and elsewhere. Her present home is in Trondheim in Norway. Vinterbo-Hohr made her debut in 1987 with her novel-length prose poem, *Palimpsest*, for which she was awarded a Norwegian prize for a first work. Since then, she has published a collection of poetry and written several essays on literary and cultural theory. Vinterbo-Hohr has taken part in several international conferences, both as speaker and as a reader of her own work. In 1992, she was Visiting Poet at the Yates Festival in Sligo, Ireland.

MY SLENDER TEACHER, with sorrow hidden in dark eyes, set in a thoughtful face, with fine penmanship and a quick reaction to everything, you were also the house-father at the boarding school. The hand that held the chalk had callouses and sores from working in the barn and potato field and with the electric generator, from rowing for provisions in the fjord community that had no roads. You, who got us to listen, even when you had to hold classes in the sleeping halls because the classrooms in the basement were flooded in the spring, I never saw you rest. You sat correcting papers by lamplight in the evening, your noble wife mended clothes, her face gray with weariness under the burden of being a mother. For twenty, thirty, forty children who needed warm food after school, dry clothes after play in the snow, kind words or scoldings, and a loving good night. Children who cried themselves to sleep and were awakened by nightmares in a strange place.

You spoke perfect Norwegian, translated fluently to Sami in church and when the sheriff, clergyman, or other authority figure descended upon sinners of various kinds. You taught me basic arithmetic and orthography. You walked miles to warn against cheap reading the student who devoured the books in the school library faster than you could supply them. Could you have even remotely imagined that the flow of slick weekly magazines and The Best of Reader's Digest and the Fredhøis Company publications that you detested was directed here with your bishop's blessing, to make us thoroughly Norwegian?

What would have happened to you if you had loaned me the collection of Sami fairytales to which you yourself had contributed? That would have saved the mother tongue for the child who read Norwegian and Sami long before she started school. But teachers before you had been reprimanded for less. You had eight children of your own. How much does the straw weigh that broke the camel's back?

They were survival experts.

They often spoke with one another only with their eyes. The convoy south would consist of fishing smacks, as many passengers as possible on each, and all would have to take turns standing on deck during bitter November days. Wool comforters were made into coats for us children; what hides that were prepared, biekso-boots and Sami brogues.

Then each picked out from among life's necessities the things they couldn't do without. A little crockery, the sewing machine, the wool carders, and the set of needles for sewing leather. Not the spinning wheel. Father's tool chest, the open one with a handle, the one he carried with him when he set up the shed and the well house; also the big one that could be locked, where everything had its place, the planes, the drills, the level.

Not the carpenter's bench.

Mother bid farewell to the cow and heifer in the Sami woman's
way, her arms wrapped around the animal's neck and her
forehead against its warm side. No one was allowed to watch, the
tears were too bitter.

Father took all the sheep and lambs, the calf, and Dokka's white
goat in his arms and carried them out of the barn, just as he would
have done any autumn.

Only a few could bring themselves to slaughter all their farm
animals. The former hunter took that responsibility upon himself,
animals must not suffer, he worked quickly and effectively. A
senseless act of destruction, he never again touched a butcher's
knife.

Featherbeds and wool comforters, no pillows. Food enough for
one week.

During the first war that was also carried out in the air, it sometimes happened that planes went into a tailspin and fell, without leaving a smoke trail behind.

The dead pilots had no bullet wounds, nor were any vital parts of the fuselage hit by projectiles.

One was faced with an enigma. Had the young men committed suicide after having won a battle between life and death?

In the final year of the war, a young medical student was drafted. He had just completed his preclinical exams and was too inexperienced to serve as a field medic. The owner of a private airplane at that, he was immediately sent to war. He won his first dog fight and headed back to the airbase.

Some seconds passed before he realized what he was seeing right in front of him: The ground was coming at him, rotating slowly. He was heading downward, all the while certain that he was flying straight ahead.

Just a few weeks earlier, he had been examined on the organ that governs equilibrium in human beings and asked to explain the Coriolis effect. As though in a dream, it dawned on him now that the very attribute that prevents dizziness when the body rotates was about to be the death of him.

While his thoughts still labored, he had corrected the course of his plane, the first of all having entered the deadly spiral to come out of it.

He was discharged; continued his studies; received his doctorate, based on his investigations of the protective mechanism that had cost so many lives; and became a professor only few years later. Then he vanished from the world of research.

He was lost for twelve years. All this time he practiced medicine in a remote village up in the mountains. Following the next war, he returned and resumed his research on problems with the human sensory apparatus. A series of strokes had damaged important muscles used in speaking. He gave lectures with the aid of larynx microphones. Rude first-year students laughed at his mask-like face. He used Christian Morgenstern to make theories understandable with the help of such paradoxes as Korff's spectacles and the olfactory pipe organ. He could be seen daily on his regular route, an old man with his white bull terrier.

From the sections "Under skriften" [Beneath the writing] and "Corioliseffekten"
[The Coriolis effect] in Palimpsest, *1987*
Translated by Edi Thorstensson in collaboration with the author.

Marry A. Somby

Let the Northern Lights Erase Your Name

Marry Ailonieida Somby (1953–) is a native of Deatnu/Tana in Norway and now lives in Tromsø. She published the first children's book in Sami, *Ámmul ja alit oarbmælli* [Ámmul and the Blue Cousin], in 1976 and has produced four more books since. Several of her books have been translated into Norwegian, and her poems originally wirtten in English have been included in anthologies published in the United States. She has studied at the University of Tromsø and worked with puppet theater. Most recently, she has written pieces for theater. Marry Somby has lived in both North and South America and thus is familiar with the American Indians' situation, which also forms the background for her first collection of poetry, the bilingual book *Krigeren, elskeren og klovnen/Mu Apache ráhkesvuohta* [The Warrior, the Lover, and the Clown].

*B*ARREN ROCK PLAINS
ringed by tall mountains
The Inca warrior snatches
a lizard
and consumes it alive

Days and nights
time runs out like shoofly liquor
from the bottoms of empty bottles
blurry talk and lashing words
clenched fists strike
batter and strike

*

Come with me
to my lavvo
my soot-stained tent
let us light
a fire
and gaze steadily
into the flames

245

*

Dressed in a wedding gown
of netted sinews
and spider's web
I step
into your canoe
waiting
at the clouds' edge
your coal-dark eyes flash
you push me from the shore
alone, I travel
far, far
to that which is not

*

May the Northern Lights
burn
your name
engulf it in flames
that flicker
as intensely
as all the silk skirts
you have touched

*

The sun
that has been away
for so long
ascends
I sprinkle rock crystals
and glass beads
from a leather pouch
tanned with alder bark
I sacrifice
to the birch tree

The bridal crown
of fluttering silk ribbons
and signs of the moon
I hang in the tree

The yoik-king and the wolf-singer
come with me
The ptarmigans are shell-white
with black-tipped wings

From Krigeren, Elskeren og Klovnen/Mu Apache Ráhkesvuohta, *1994*
Translated by Edi Thorstensson

Ailo Gaup

The Night Between the Days

Ailo Gaup (1944–) is from Guovdageaidnu/Kautokeino in Finnmark, but he lives in Oslo. Gaup worked for many years as a journalist for one of Norway's largest newspapers, but today he is a full-time creative writer. He has published both collections of poetry and novels and has written a musical, commissioned by Beaivváš Sami theater. The title of this musical is *Min duoddarat* [Our Land]. Gaup made his debut as a novelist in 1988, when *Trommereisen* [In Search of the Drum] was published. *Natten mellom dagene* [Night between the Days] can be regarded as its sequel; it is a novel in which the hero, Jon, travels from Oslo to Sapmi with the intention of making a drum for himself.

$\mathcal{T}$HREE DAYS OF DRIVING and 2,000 kilometers lay behind them; they were almost there.

Jon turned off the main road and down into the dusk of the valley, where they were headed. Karin had drawn a map for them and they found the house. Lajla unlocked and walked through the unfamiliar rooms. They were tired. They washed up and went to bed.

"My God, how wonderful to lie down. Imagine not having a bed," Lajla said. Both of them fell asleep at once.

The next morning he carried their things in from the car. She helped him with the darkroom equipment. It fit in the laundry room. He put his box in a corner of the house.

"Where should I put this lamp?" Lajla asked as he came in with the last box. "You have to look at me. Look here," she said in that alluring way she had. "Is this good?"

"Yes."

"Perhaps it should go further into the corner?" Lajla pushed the wall lamp into the corner of the room.

"I think it looks better where you had it first," Jon said.

"No, this is where it should be," she decided, found a screw and attached the lamp.

"The car is empty. Everything is inside." Jon leaned against the doorjamb.

"Good."

Lajla pulled his box out from the corner and put a chair in the light of the lamp.

"That's good, isn't it?" she said. She was the one responsible for the decorating.

"I came here to make myself a drum. Why did you come along?" Jon asked.

"I came because of you," Lajla answered. "And because I love to be close to nature and have light and views around me."

"So that's why you chose this narrow valley far north of the Arctic Circle at a time of year when the sun soon disappears and darkness sets in." His feelings for her were warm. He just did not like her taking his box out of the corner.

"I want a change. I was tired of traffic jams and shopping lines. Even out in the woods surrounding the city, we walked in lines," Lajla continued.

She opened another cardboard box, took out a piece of hand-printed cloth and looked around for a place to hang it. She said Indians lived inside the pattern, but Jon never discovered them.

"Is there something else I can do?" he asked.

"No, you have done your part. The rest is my job," she answered.

"Well, I'm going to have a look around, then."

"Do that. Go out and get acquainted with the place. I can't relax until I've tidied everything up in here and in the darkroom."

Full of a giddy and unusual expectation, Jon sat down in the car.

*

The house they had rented was situated by itself along the road that went through the community. Further down, there was a house and a concrete block building that was painted white. When he drove past it, he saw that it was a garage. Other houses could be seen behind the fields along the road. Where the road ended, there were two farms.

Jon turned around, drove back, past their new home and across a small bridge. A black dog came running like a shot out of a driveway and ran barking after the car.

He passed the school. Children waved in the windows.

The center of the community consisted of the intersection of the two roads, a church, a country store with gas pumps, a post office, and a stand with clothing and boots for sale.

The country road followed the valley floor through a birch forest. The first house that appeared was fairly new. The house was located on the left-hand side, with the gable end facing the road. Outside, there were two cars and a *lavvo*. Reindeer pelts were nailed up to dry on the shed wall.

High up on the slopes, farms and houses were spread out among the fields. Altogether, the road was three or four kilometers long. Another road connected the houses higher up to the main road.

The main road came from the south, through Finland, and continued northward to the coast. It rose in a slight curve up across the side of the valley. There was a turnoff on the right hand side that led to a café. He passed it now but stopped at a turnoff at the highest viewpoint overlooking the whole valley.

It was a quiet and beautiful September day, with a soft wind and inviting sun over the valley and the river. A sharp peak pointed its nose up in the air on the opposite side of the valley, like a landmark over the surrounding area.

What would this year bring? Would he make himself a magic drum, like the one the old shamans had?

It was to make a drum that he had come here – learn from it, from nature, and from the starry skies. Yet he was curious to discover whom he would meet. He would pay special attention to the first conversations he had with the locals.

Outside the store, an ATV with four wide balloon tires was parked between a couple of cars. Mostly women and children were inside. The children cast curious glances at him, the stranger getting milk, bread, sandwich meats, and thinly sliced reindeer meat. The cashier was a dark girl who barely looked up.

As he drove home, he met the first pedestrian. It was a small woman with a walking stick, and she walked all the way out on the edge of the road.

Now he wanted to explore the unknown landscape on foot.

Two yelping dogs raced along at his heels, but they lost interest when he turned onto a path. On a ledge up on the slope he found the remains of a fire in a ring of stones. In the bottom of a narrow hollow, a small creek gurgled. The ravine narrowed between the mountain sides. Had that small river gouged this out?

On a shoulder-high shelf, a birch had taken root in what amounted to a bucketful of soil.

He had heard and read that the noaidi, the old shamans, looked for ravines and gorges. That is where they searched for the outgrowths and birch burls they needed for bowl drums. The trees should preferably have grown where no other trees had taken root, in rugged terrain far from other trees of the same kind. Although this small birch was not useful, it was a heroic and courageous tree.

Above the deep ravine was a level area with a small lake between the peaks. Reindeer hooves had made a path. A pale bone shone on the path.

In a pit between a couple of stones, he saw a white animal skull with a row of teeth in the jaw and empty eye sockets. Here the head and the bones had been left behind, while the rest of the animal had been taken home to the stew pot. The horn had been left behind, too, and Jon took it.

By the river he found a path leading up toward the houses on top. In a bow of the river, by the singing water, he sat down in the heather. The sun was blessed with warmth, and the afternoon was peaceful. He had done it. He had liberated himself from the hold of the city and the stress of the newspaper job. First he had to feel grounded. Then he wanted to take the time that was needed to find the raw material for the bowl drum.

A person in a jogging suit came toward him on the path. It was a small, round man with a small, round stomach, round face, round cheeks and eyes. Even his ears were round. The man's name was Anders. He was a colleague of Karin's; they both worked in the school. They sat down, talked about the beautiful weather, the first fall colors, and the horn Jon had found.

"What are you going to do here?" Anders asked.

"I want to learn traditional crafts, use my hands, and work with wood."

"What do you want to make?"

"Traditional things – wooden cups and things like that – perhaps a Sami knife," Jon answered.

"I teach traditional woodworking, and I give evening classes, too."

"Are there any birch burls on the trees around here?" Jon asked.

"This area has been picked clean. I usually look for raw materials down south when I am there."

Anders stood up, wiped his clothes clean from grass and heather.

"Do you make other things, too?" Jon asked, as he, too, stood up.

"I make most of the things that they made and used in the old days – from knives to cradleboards, sleds, and small log buildings, if you need that."

"There is something else I would like to have. Perhaps you could help me with it?"

"A river boat perhaps?" Anders asked.

"No, a drum."

"A noaidi drum?" Anders asked, and Jon nodded.

"No one around here makes them."

"Does no one use them anymore?" Jon asked.

"No one around here. Who knows what would happen if you tried? What would you do if the Devil came flying?" Anders hesitated before continuing. "I have heard Johan say that he dares. He lives out by the coast."

Lajla was beginning to get the house and the darkroom in order.

So now they were really here. She had lost the land of their ancestors as an 18 year-old, and that was 18 years ago now.

256

She was pleased to have 150 kilometers of country road between her and the homestead. Anything less she would not have wanted, for when she left, she had vowed never to come back.

While she was frying the thinly sliced reindeer meat, Mother Maja appeared out of nowhere and stood in front of her as if alive. Mother Maja, in her own calm way, had helped her to leave home. Now it was as if she welcomed her back.

They ate a late dinner and celebrated moving in with candles and a bottle of red wine.

"By the way, what do you have to say, you who have been out in the big, wide world?" Lajla asked.

"I drove up and down the road. Altogether I saw 100 houses, a few *lavvos*, a store, a church, a school, five dogs, a couple of farms, a café, and a small old woman with a walking stick."

"What did you see in the forest?"

"I hiked up over the ridge and down along the river. I saw a ravine, trees, stones, and nightfall. I met a man named Anders who teaches woodworking. He knows how to make all kinds of things out of wood. But he knows very little about drums."

"Don't expect too much. I'm warning you again."

"He was afraid that the Devil himself would leap out of the drum. Imagine that."

"You know what Christianity did to the older generations. They had to forget the noaidi arts in order to survive."

"I know about burning people at the stake and the executioner's axe, but that's history and a long time ago now," Jon answered.

"My dear man, fear is still widespread today, even if the times are milder and the means gentler than before. Ministers and preachers do what they can to hold people in their grip – I thought you understood that."

257

"Anders mentioned someone named Johan, who lives out by the coast. According to Anders, Johan apparently dares to use a drum. Can you imagine that?"

"Don't complain. He gave you a clue," Lajla answered as she went into the bathroom to get ready for the night.

There was a lamp hook in the bedroom ceiling that was not being used. Lajla did not feel it was necessary for a lamp to hang in the middle of the ceiling. To her, lamps should be placed in the corners, or on the walls. Jon tied a colored ribbon around the horn and hung it on the hook.

When Lajla came in from the bathroom, she did not voice any objections. She just nodded slightly to his idea before she crawled in under the comforter.

"Does that enthusiastic response mean that my contribution to the decoration is accepted?"

"Yes," she answered briefly, before her thoughts continued on another course. Even in a *lavvo*, people had their own places to sleep. Even homeless people in the asphalt jungles of New York fought to keep their paper bag. Imagine what it would be like to live without one's own bed. "Are you not going to bed soon?" she finally asked.

"Not yet. I am going outside to look at the stars."

No one else was outside. Not even a dog sniffed around.
He followed the road down to where it ended. His feet found the path that continued along the river's edge.

He had traveled to his ancestor's land because the drums of the tribe called. He needed grounding. He needed darkness. Perhaps he also needed winter.

He stood by the singing river that ran right through the sleeping landscape.

Surrounded by the dark, northern night, he looked for a sign from his guiding-star high up in the sky.

*

What Anders had said was true. The forest in the surrounding area was picked clean. If he was to find any raw material, he would have to go where people rarely traveled. Jon bought a hatchet, stuck it in his backpack with some food, a cooking pot, rain gear, and a sleeping bag.

It was early in the morning, the trees were still covered with hoarfrost when he took off down through the settlement. Where the road ended, he continued along the path. The ground was frozen, ice flowers covered the water puddles.

He passed pastures, hay fields, and a collapsed hay barn.

Where the path vanished, Jon continued along the shore. He walked on sand, jumped across muddy holes, and climbed over fallen trees. When he pushed his way through dense brush, the buzz of insects rose from the ground.

A tributary had cut its way through a narrow gorge. He looked for raw material for his drum there, but the trees were too small. The burl he was looking for had to be larger than a soccer ball, about the size of a cradleboard. He was a hunter in the morning light. He roamed up and down along the rolling mountain side, scouting for his prey, while silently praying that the earth and the forest would give him what he needed.

The river flowed wide and sluggish toward the sea.

There was an island out in the water.

Large birches grew out there.

They had to be checked out.

He took off his rubber boots and socks. The water was cold, but not ice cold.

The island was not more than twenty paces long and ten paces wide, and in the middle of it was an open place surrounded by trees. They were happy, beautiful birches, but they did not have what he was looking for.

He made a fire, boiled water for some tea, and ate.

As the fire died, he dozed off on top of his sleeping bag.

An almost imperceptible wind lifted him up from the valley, up on a cloud. On it, he sailed far, farther than far, into the blue light of the sky. This was a game, of course, a grownup game in the realm of fantasy. Through the blue light, a ray of sunshine arrived. He rode on it to a land of light, where magical animals waited. He had played with reindeer before. But now a shining wolf came over the ridge. It took him in its jaws and could not be controlled. With long leaps and at a breakneck speed, it took off. The wolf suddenly stopped and released him in an unknown place in the snow, in front of a woman dressed in skins.

"Welcome," she said with a clear voice and patted the wolf, stroking its shining fur. They began playing together, so that snow crystals began to twinkle and whirl around them like stars in the night sky. It occurred to him that this was not just a fantasy. He was in the middle of a great dream.

"I brought you here," the woman said. She was suddenly right in front of him.

"What do you want of me?"

"You are to learn about the dreams of the darkness and the power of winter. Snow, cold, and darkness is good for nature, and it is good for you."

"Who are you?" he asked.

"I am Safia, daughter of the Hoarfrost Man." The woman

laughed. While she laughed, a whirling wind began to blow around her. When the snow settled again, Safia was gone.

The water from the big river had cut a narrow, v-shaped gorge through the mountain. The stones along the shore were covered with ice. This was a place where one could easily fall and break a leg or an ankle. A broken river boat was wedged between some boulders in the current.

The path vanished, and the likelihood of being able to pass along the shore was difficult to gauge. Would he have to retrace his steps now or climb all the way up to the top of the high and steep ravine? He did not want to do it. A boat would have been perfect.

A horizontal crack gave him a foothold in the mountain. With his stomach pressed against the rock and his fingers in tiny cracks, he managed to move sideways in over the chasm. A damp, cold wind rose from the dark current below him.

Then the crack narrowed, and there was less and less space for his feet. His heels hung over the edge and his backpack pulled him backwards.

Would it be possible to move forward? Or should he turn before it was too late? He took another couple of careful sidesteps and noticed that the hold was slight under his toes.

He saw a shelf below, to which he would be able to slide down and be saved. But the rock face arched, so that he could not see if the shelf continued or if it simply was a trap to get caught in, like a lost sheep.

He hung, like one crucified, on the wet mountain wall. His strength began to fade. His fingers were stiff and cold, and his thigh muscles hurt from the unnatural strain. It was the moment when a professional climber would have hammered a bolt into the rock wall and rappelled himself down to safety.

261

He should have brought a boat along with his gear.

The shelf sloped wide and safe toward the outlet of a ravine. A new body of water spread out in front of his eyes. Treetops stuck up from the surface. Whole trees stood below the water's mirror, like ghosts in the current.

He walked along the artificial shore for a while, then started sideways up across the ridge. The entire valley formed a peculiar basin.

At the time when everything began, a noaidi had said that the dam would never be built. Machines and workers would not be able to pass a certain boulder on the mountain. They would be held back by invisible forces. On the tundras of the Sapmi, reindeer and ptarmigan would reign.

From the novel Natten mellom dagene, *1992*
Translated by Lars Nordström

Stig Gælok

They Don't Know Our Songs

Stig Gælok (1961–) is from Tysfjord in Nordland. Thus, he writes in Lule Sami, which is the middle of the three main Sami dialects in Norway. The Sami cultural divisions do not follow national borders but rather cut across them, so that Lule Sami is also spoken in adjacent areas on the Swedish side of the border. The other two dialects are Northern Sami – spoken by the majority of Sami people – and Southern Sami, which is found in the southernmost part of the Sami settlement region in both Norway and Sweden. Stig Gælok is a poet who has chosen to include parallel Norwegian text in his more recent books, so that they can reach a larger reading public, beyond the small group that understands Lule Sami. Gælok's first book; *O, Oarjjevuodna*, published in 1983, was the first book of poetry to be published in Lule Sami.

*T*HE WIND WHISTLES
the old one's lament
can you hear?

warmth is felt
through hearts
one more night together
with love

in the breast
the heart beats
pumping blood
through the body

arteries

warm blood in your hands

*

when the earth
had rotated
twice

then it came
into sight
in the sun
and my own
sea gull's
fetus
fell
into its nest

*

then we cried
there
and were cried over
were happy
and were, in turn, rejoiced
we had
even in
those days
begun to limp
we didn't dare
believe
it was true
when our parents
asked that we
return
to their fold

*

there
we lowered
this

266

destitute
little bird
into the cradle
where
the carnivors
no longer
reach

*

many times
I believed
in those days
I was
foolish
was convinced
that their steel
murdered
didn't know
the knife
from my own
belt
in my hands
didn't notice
before I began
to cut
my own
sinews

From "Vuonak"/"–…fra fjordene", *1986*
and "–ale desti"/"–ikke mer!", *1992*
Translated by Edi Thorstensson

Inger-Mari Aikio

So Fed Up with This Life

Inger-Mari Aikio (1961–) was born in Norway but grew up in Ohcejohka, on the Finnish side of the border. She has studied at the university in Oulu in Finland and works with Finnish Sami radio broadcasting in Anár/Inari. Ima, as she is popularly called, is a cosmopolitan and usually spends half of each year traveling about in the world. Occasionally, travel motifs find expression in her writing, but for the most part she takes her themes from the Sami environment and from her own experiences. *Silkeguobbara lákca*, 1995, [The Silk Mushroom's Cream] is her third poetry collection and most recent work.

*S*O FED UP
with this life

I sit near the back
of the airplane
there the chances
of survival
are greatest

       *

after all the axe-men
playing fingers
like grass breathing

and I rang
all night long

       *

I will come at six o'clock!

have to find time to wash up
make up
tidy up

bake
make tea
set the table

everything ready
long before six
in high spirits
happy

soon
soon now
surely quite soon

soon
surely quite soon

*

for the second time already

I am not waiting
a third time

I am no longer
18 years old

*

272

the fingers that play
did not return

the wolves howled
all night long

     *

that person is blessed
who does not wish to own
but why
is it my fate
to always just borrow

     *

don't speak of love

after one night.
I, too, am silent
speaking only
when you have gone

     *

the rain lashes the asphalt
presses my wet hair
against my breasts
even the last swallow
has flown north
oh, loneliness!

     *

lie to me
deceive me

you will be my poems

*

in your senses
birch leaves
familiar but
when I taste you
it stings like acid on my tongue
my throat burns

*

the young birch doesn't ask the time
it has a sea of time.

the tree asks the time
and estimates
when its sap will lose its sweet taste

the dead pine doesn't ask for the time
it has a sea of time

*

you are a safe thought
that appears blue in the distance
I wrap myself in your light

but the sun no longer rose
its rays went out
the blue was suffocated in darkness

my time was lost
I forgot to breathe
from barren land smoke rises

*

between the clouds
I set the sinker.
climb up the long-line
above the birch branches
wave to the ants
with my ring finger.
thanks and good-bye.

From Gollebiekkat almmi dievva, *1989*
and Jiehkki vuolde ruonas gidda, *1992*
Translated by Edi Thorstensson

Notes on the translators

Edi Thorstensson (b. 1944), B.A. in Norwegian Language and Literature, St. Olaf College. M.A. in Library Science, University of Minnesota. Free-lance translator and weaver. Lives in St. Peter, Minnesota.

Roland Thorstensson (b. 1946), Ph.D. in Scandinavian Studies, University of Washington, Seattle. Associate Professor in Scandinavian Studies and Swedish at Gustavus Adolphus College, St. Peter, Minnesota.

Lars Nordström (b. 1954), Ph.D. in American Literature from Uppsala University. Free-lance translator and author. Lives on a vineyard in Beavercreek, Oregon, USA, with his wife and two sons.

Pekka Sammallahti (b. 1947), Ph.D., Professor of Sami Language and Culture, University of Oulu, Finland, and adjunct Professor of Sami Language at the University of Tromsø, Norway. Has published several books and articles on Sami language and Uralic linguistics. Translates into Sami, Finnish and English from various languages.

Gerd Bjørhovde (b. 1943), Dr.philos., Professor of English Literature, University of Tromsø. Has published several books and articles on 19th and 20th century women writers. In recent years a special interest has been so-called "post-colonial" writing, more specifically indigenous women writers from several parts of the world.

Ralph Salisbury (b. 1926), Professor Emeritus at the Department of English at the University of Oregon, Eugene, and a Native American author. Has published several books of poems and is widely anthologized. His newest book is a collection of short stories, *One Indian and Two Chiefs*, 1993. Lives with his poet wife, Ingrid Wendt, in Eugene, Oregon.

Harald Gaski (b. 1955), Associate Professor in Sami Literature at the University of Tromsø, and the author and editor of several books and articles on Sami Literature and Culture. Fortcoming in English is a collection of articles on contemporary Sami cultural matters, *Sami Culture in a New Era: The Norwegian Sami Experience*.